A Boy From Aruba
a memoir

Piet H. van Ogtrop

Piet H. van Ogtrop

Copyright © 2024 Piet H. van Ogtrop

Cover art by Michaela Penkala

Background photo by Lex Melony on Unsplash

All rights reserved

ISBN: 978-0-9976309-4-7

A Boy From Aruba

To my life partner and the love of my life, Connie: many thanks for your support and love and your doggedness in keeping our ship of life upright and on course. Your "crew" of our three daughters provided and continues to provide immeasurable help and love to us both.

Piet H. van Ogtrop

A Boy From Aruba

CONTENTS

Author's Note		1
Prologue		3
1	Life in Aruba	5
2	Trips to Holland	7
3	College in Cleveland	9
4	Eagles Mere	13
5	Boston College Law School	15
6	Connie in Aruba, 1961	17
7	Life in Carlisle	19
8	Young Parents in Newark	23
9	Initial Home Ownership	25
10	A Home in the Country	29
11	Subsequent Homes	35
12	Boalsburg	39
13	Residency at Foxdale	41
14	My Legal Career	43
15	Various Sports	55
16	Vacations and Trips	69

Piet H. van Ogtrop

A Boy From Aruba

17 Friends	73
18 Random Remembrances	75
19 Dedicated to My Family	81
20 Conclusion	95
Acknowledgment	101
About the Author	103

Piet H. van Ogtrop

A Boy From Aruba

Author's Note

Life is a quality that distinguishes a vital and functional being from inanimate matter and is characterized by experiences which are capable of perception. I consider life to be a series of stages: the beginning, the midpoint and the end. I have experienced all three, from the beginning (birth in 1939 until September 7, 1956, bound for the United States and college); to the middle stage (college, law school, marriage, parenthood, legal career and retirement in January 2012); to the third and final stage (January 2012 until the day I am bound for a different place).

This "document" contains references to persons, places and things in the various stages, perhaps not in sequential order, but as I recollect them, and my successes and failures in each stage. I have had many wonderful experiences, along with some mishaps. All in all, upon reflection, my life has been filled with blessings and to steal the well-known adage from time immemorial, I have had a life well lived.

I do not know whether this document is an autobiography, memoir or biography. I'll call it a memoir as it places on paper a recollection of events, places, persons and things which have been stored away in my memory bank.

I have never written a memoir and am therefore not on solid ground to defend this document, but all of you who believe it to be too boastful, self aggrandizing or narcissistic, either stop reading it or indulge me.

Piet H. van Ogtrop

A Boy From Aruba

Prologue

I understand a memoir to be a compilation of an author's stories and events that had meaning to the author and can be grouped as a series of chapters in the author's life, and it is in that context that I approach this series of "chapters" in my life, which life has been full of treasures, pleasures and experiences and which have permitted me to say that I have had a life fully lived. I have attempted to create a chronology of times and dates as much as I can recall them, but try as I might, there is no way to create a chronological sequence as there is not a meshing of experiences to make that practical.

Research I have engaged in suggests that a memoir should lead off with a laugh, and also suggests that experiences can be the subject of anecdotes, as well as real life experiences. Accordingly, my entry into the world on February 24, 1939 is an anecdotal experience in which I participated, with no "input," only "output," from me. My dear parents were fervent Catholics and presumably did not engage in pre-marital hanky-panky, and I was made aware through anecdotal evidence that I was conceived ten minutes out at sea on a ship leaving Holland for Aruba where my father, a doctor who had done his residency in Holland with emphasis on Urology, was to embark on a career with Exxon (formerly Esso) at a large hospital in the Urology Department. My parents were married on May 3, 1938 and left Holland on May 4, 1938, solely referenced for context. In days of old, a bastard was considered an illegitimate person. If the reader does the math, the time between May 4, 1938 and February 24, 1939, (my date of birth) exceeds nine months and so my legitimacy is not in dispute. A bastard is also defined in Webster as a disagreeable person, a very broad definition indeed. As I was my mother's first of seven children and I came out feet first and weighed eight pounds and four ounces, I am sure she disliked the little bastard she carried for nine months, although she never "punished" me for that. So, the math made me legitimate and my post-birth experiences and behavior to some may have made them think of me as disagreeable. If so, then I submit that I am only one-half bastard.

Those smarter than me who are associated with memoir-writing suggest writing memories and experiences in chapter form and that is the approach I use. The chapters will each be devoted to different experiences and events, and rather than trying to weave all of them into a story, I will simply list in each chapter meaningful memories which I have had the pleasure or displeasure of having been engaged in or being the recipient thereof. The length of the chapters is governed by time spent in the matters discussed, the extent of the experiences and relationships, and consequently each chapter will be different in length.

Chapter 1
Life in Aruba: Pre-college and Experiences

I fondly remember the following:

- family outings to Sea Grape Groves for picnics
- sumptuous Sunday night dinners on the patio with post-meal creme de menthe for my mother after another good meal
- chaos at dinnertime with yelling by family members at delivery people
- swimming on Christmas mornings after going to friends' homes for spiked eggnog
- climbs to Mt. Hooiberg
- trips to the principal's office for misbehaving in Miss Gallicani's Spanish class
- breaking into Mr. Krebs classroom with Billy Johnson, a.k.a. "Gator," to "swipe" the physics exam off his desk so that I would not get an F in my senior year
- spending one evening in jail for Halloween pranks with Billy Johnson and other dudes
- getting Fs in conduct for being class clown, talking too much in class, being disruptive and mischievous
- playing golf on a nine-hole course with sand greens
- taking HATED Dutch lessons on Tuesdays
- backing the family car into a ditch behind the hospital while playing hanky-panky with my girlfriend Lulu Koopman
- frequent night beach parties
- sneaking over to the bowling alley to reserve ball number one and hiding it in the rafters

- going to confession every two weeks to confess sins (of which there were many in the "old days")
- hitting a home run with bases loaded in a crucial baseball game against the better team from Oranjestad, but only getting a triple as George Turner — Coach — yelled, "van Ogtrop, you run fast but stay in one place too long"
- going to the village after hours to drink beer
- Saturday matinees and "necking" with my various girlfriends
- driving the old Ford, a.k.a. the Blue Bitch, in a contest with my siblings and turning off the engine and letting it glide some yards down the road to see how close we could get it to the palm tree across the road from our home
- Sunday morning Mass, kneeling on hard pews and having my mother, who was proud of her seven kids, walk up the main aisle of St. Theresa Church
- kneeling around our folks' bed in HEAVENLY airconditioned comfort
- saying the rosary during Lent
- playing softball games at night with my brothers and hearing my mother hooting and hollering from the stands, while my dad, perhaps mortified, walked in the outfield under the shadows so as not to be associated with the crazy lady who had no compunctions about calling out "nice catch, Dittle, you bum!" when Jock Dittle dropped an easy fly ball

The list could go on and on but it would be too long. My life was a blast on our little island paradise and I have much more to relate.

Chapter 2
Various Trips to Holland

Some memories of visits to Holland stand out. On one occasion, all seven kids stayed with my parents at my grandfather's home — my mother's dad — and he had a beautiful vegetable garden and yard. My two brothers and I played softball in his yard and ruined it and the vegetable garden and we were characterized by my grandfather as the "savages from Aruba." On a separate occasion, the same grandfather asked me to translate from Dutch into English a treatise on chemical issues (he was a chemist) and after one session he thought better of it as I did not "know my ass from a hole in the ground." He thought I could speak enough Dutch to help him but that was not the case. I can still speak enough Dutch to get by.

An additional trip in the 1980s to Holland to celebrate our twenty-fifth wedding anniversary, suggested and planned by our three daughters, was highlighted by meeting cousins for the first time and renewing some relationships with other cousins from previous visits, in 1954 and 1957, I believe. One of my favorite cousins, along with her twin brother Dolf, asked Connie and me to go out for a coffee, which we did. The wait person asked me if I wanted my coffee "with or without," and I inquired of my cousin what that meant. "Marijuana in your coffee, of course," she said. I declined. whereupon she exclaimed, "You Americans are so provincial!" She was a character and she, Dolf, their younger brother and their mother — my father's sister, Maria — all survived four years in a Japanese concentration camp in Sumatra in WWII, while her husband and their father served in the Dutch Navy.

I am proud of my Dutch heritage and the resilience of the Dutch, notwithstanding their philosophy of "anything goes." History has shown that conservative behavior is not prevalent in their collective DNA.

Piet H. van Ogtrop

Chapter 3
College in Cleveland, Ohio, 1956–60

My parents thought a Jesuit education was very appropriate, as my father's brother was a Jesuit priest. My mother did all the work associated with getting me into John Carroll University starting on September 7, 1956, as I cared only about playing sports, with occasional studying, in high school. I left Aruba on a ship with classmates who were going to various colleges and we had a great time. I arrived in New York City to meet Carol Garber, the daughter of my mother's best friend, who took me shopping for winter clothes, etc., including my first fancy suit from a company called Rogers, Peet & Co. I never knew fancy clothes cost so much, as they were not a necessity in Aruba.

I flew from La Guardia to Hopkins Airport in Cleveland, Ohio with fifty dollars in my pocket for my September allowance. I landed in Cleveland, knew no one, had no one to meet me and knew nothing about busses, trains or other modes of transportation. Aruba is just nineteen miles long and six miles wide, so "fancy" transportation was not heard of, particularly for a young person. Not knowing better, I took a cab, which cost me twenty-four of my fifty dollars. I entered room seven in Pacelli Hall, extended my hand to my roommate and did not receive a response. He had taken the lower bunk in our room, the s---head. I was hungry and needed to conserve my money, as my meal plan didn't start for two more days. I went to bed and while I did not cry myself to sleep, I wanted my mom and dad.

My first meal in Cleveland was pie a la mode: apple pie and chocolate ice cream, and a chocolate milk shake the following day. Welcome to the real world, Island Boy! I had a new roommate two weeks or so later from Chicago (my first roommate left school after three days and was evidently bipolar). I went home with him one weekend and bought a winter coat on Maxwell Street (all "hot" stuff, as Maxwell Street was Mafia-run) for eight dollars and wore it all four years.

Piet H. van Ogtrop

I will impart three additional memorable experiences. I was hired at a local pizza parlor, but was fired the end of the first day as I put too much cheese and sauce on the pizza. I also flunked compulsory Military Science. On my first day on the drill field in early January 1957, with my rifle on my shoulder and my uniform on, in twenty-degree weather, I decided this was not for me and I never went out again. I had to take the course my second semester in 1960 to graduate.

One last laugh clearly indicates how "wet behind the ears" this foreigner was. My first trip out of Ohio was to Pittsburgh with my friend Tom Sabow, who had a car and was driving. I was in the back seat with Mickey Tegano. Jim Keim rode in the front passenger seat. I handed Tom my green card (I was still a Dutch citizen and became a U.S. citizen in 1962) and passport at the toll booth. He exclaimed, "What are these?" And I, knowing no better, said, "We are going to a new state and think you'll need them." "Where are you from, Mars?" asked Tom. "This is the U.S.A.!" Welcome to the big leagues, Dutchie!

Graduation from John Carrroll in Cleveland;
with Tom Sabow

Many other fond memories in Ohio: the first snow I ever saw; many Cleveland Browns and Indians home games; and graduating on time, albeit not as a distinguished student. My college experience was positive and typical of a young man in college in the late 1950s and early 1960s. I majored in history and minored in political science, and the next step in the progression was going to law school, not to become a famous barrister but to evade the draft, which I suspect many other college graduates also similarly did. I did receive a deferment until about September 18, 1963 to take the Delaware bar exam. More on that in succeeding chapters.

Piet H. van Ogtrop

Chapter 4
Eagles Mere: Vacation and Good Fortune, Summer 1960

My parents were entitled to take at least a two-month vacation every three years away from Aruba. They combined my college graduation with their vacation in the Alleghenies in LaPorte, Pennsylvania in a cottage owned by one of my father's colleagues from Aruba, seven or so miles from Eagles Mere, a summer resort. The three van Ogtrop brothers found employment in Eagles Mere, which had three fancy hotels then in existence. I worked as a busboy, grunt, etc. at the Lakeside Hotel. Brother John was a lifeguard at Forest Inn. Brother Bernard (whom we all called Dick and do to this day, as "dik" in Dutch means fat and he was, as a youngster) was also at Forest Inn, setting pins in the bowling alley. I do not remember what my four sisters did.

Two pretty young girls from Delaware, Lois Jones (on whom I had a HUGE crush but who rebuffed my attentions) and Connie Schmidt, also worked at the Lakeside. Over the course of the summer, Connie and I enjoyed each other's company and we were "dating," with trips to the ice cream shop every night, parties with other employees, going swimming with Judy (also a DE girl) and Wilson in the local creeks and swimming holes and generally having fun.

I initially told Connie I was from California and that I was Pete, perhaps embarrassed that she would not have known where Aruba was and also would not have known a "Piet." She finally got the true story from me and called her mom and sister in DE and advised them that she had become friendly with a boy from "the islands." Well, they came up to check me out to make sure I was not some dude swinging from the vines in the jungle or a like kind of fellow. I think I passed muster, as evidenced by further disclosure in this memoir. We had a good time that summer and as I was the only one old enough to buy beer and liquor, I would go to the liquor stores, buy beer and cheap gin or whiskey, and our group would sit in the middle of Route 42 in

Eagles Mere and party after work. We were periodically visited by the police and scattered hither and yon, but were never arrested or detained, praise God. After an enjoyable summer enjoying being with Connie, we parted company, as I was on my way to Boston College Law School and she, Lois and Judy back to Newark, Delaware to start their junior year at the University of Delaware. I never anticipated, nor perhaps neither did she, the series of events which followed and which resulted in the good fortune identified in the heading of this chapter, and identified further in this memoir. The Lakeside Hotel permanently closed at the end of that summer and the building no longer exists.

Chapter 5
Boston and Boston College Law School

I do not remember how I travelled to Boston to commence my first year of law school there in September 1960 or how I made the arrangements to become a tenant of the spinster sisters, Miss Ellis and Miss Turner. I believe that I took a huge step and made the arrangements myself. The ladies owned a large home in Newton, Massachusetts at 24 Spooner Road, and had rooms for three tenants: me, Bob Burns (a school teacher) and Jack LeBrun (an aspiring doctoral candidate at Boston College). We shared a common bathroom, a tub (no shower permitted) and limited access to the amenities.

The sisters were Catholic and if I drove them to the 7:30 a.m. Mass on Sundays, I could use the kitchen from 8:45 to 9:30 to cook my oatmeal. Sometime after settling down in Newton, I wrote to Connie in Delaware. She wrote back and we began to feel, presumably mutually, that we might become more than friends. She did in fact come to visit me on one occasion and I went to DE, I believe, and stayed at her home in Newark where her parents lived. Connie and I corresponded frequently by mail and telephone and knew we had genuine feelings and love for each other, which made my decision to transfer to Dickinson Law School in Carlisle, Pennsylvania, in September 1961, a foregone conclusion, as I had been accepted there and that story will follow.

I often walked to Boston College Law School some two to three miles away. I ate where I could near the law school and generally lived a hermit-type life as a fledgling law student. Howard Bergman became a friend and often he would pick me up for school which was a lifesaver in the winter months. The spinster sisters made it very clear to me that, upon Connie's visit, we were not to share the same bedroom or bed — HORRORS and a flagrant violation of the sixth commandment if we acted contrary to their edict!

I eventually left Boston and Connie and I went to Aruba together in the summer of 1961 (we must have become serious) and more on that later. All in all, my BC education was good and fulfilled my parents' unannounced wish that I continued being a Jesuit-schooled person.

Chapter 6
Connie in Aruba, Summer 1961

After leaving Boston College Law School and prior to moving to Carlisle to attend Dickinson Law School to begin my second year, Connie and I went to Aruba so that she could become accustomed to me and my family. She was noticeably thinner when she returned to U.S., exclaimed her mother. Small wonder! We both worked for Summer Recreation, she with small children and me with baseball, soccer and "men-type sports."

Connie came from a small family: her mom, dad and sister (married and living elsewhere), and was not used to the tumult, chaos, noise, disruptions and particularly the meal sessions. She slept in one of the bedrooms with one of my sisters and for the three brothers to get to their bedroom, we had to walk through Connie's room. Brother John was a mischievous fellow and kept playing pranks, passing gas in her dresser drawer and other silly and annoying things. All three brothers were chauvinistic enough with her that she could retaliate when able, i.e., putting salt in Brother Bernard's ice cream, and presumably other things I do not recollect. One thing for certain — Connie was not going to kowtow to her prospective husband and his brothers.

Connie and my mother enjoyed each other and would have a gin and tonic in the afternoon before our evening meal (we had our hot meal at noon) of sandwiches or other like food, such as Dinty Moore stew, Spam and other "hearty foods" to serve seven children, certainly not gourmet but nutritious enough, and washed down with powdered milk known as KLIM, as milk from the U.S. came periodically and was too costly to satisfy the needs of seven kids. One evening while enjoying a pre-meal cocktail, a scorpion crawled onto Connie and stung her on her breast, the ULTIMATE INSULT associated with her baptism by fire with the van Ogtrop "savages." She came back to the States bloodied but unbowed and returned to the University of Delaware for her senior year. I went to Carlisle for my second year of law school.

Piet H. van Ogtrop

Chapter 7
Law School Career and Life in Carlisle

I will write this chapter without any weaving of experiences into a chronological sequence but reference experiences as I remember them. I began and completed my second year in Carlisle as a single man as we were not married until June 30, 1962. I lived in the Sadler Curtilege with Ed Hines and Lance Lewis, both of whom did not finish the first semester, and I then lived alone in the all-male dorm. Periodically one of my classmates would bring "ladies of the night" to the dorm and one morning, while standing before the mirror shaving, sans clothing, and chatting with Jerry Batt, a stall door opened, and the lady exclaimed from the throne "good morning!"

I ate dinner at Dickinson Theta Chi House, with John Bowman, one of my best friends, and others, and the *quid pro quo* was that we had to do the dishes. The food was not home cooking but much better than the "jitterbug" (an order of French fries and a scoop of baked beans) from the H.A. Milton (Hamilton Hotel and pool hall), where I had lunch daily for thirty-five cents.

Barry Gwinn, who became head of the FBI in Phoenix, played pool every day with the locals and thus financed his way through school. He graduated from Gettysburg College, wore his khaki ROTC shirt at least three days in a row, turning it and his underwear and socks inside out, and was the one who introduced us to Theta Chi House, as well as the infamous jitterbugs. Gwinn borrowed John Bowman's golf shoes, removed the spikes and wore them every day until we graduated. He also used Bowman's old 1953 Buick and would drive into Harrisburg to see a telephone operator who he befriended, all the while being engaged to a lovely girl from the Main Line whose dad had a huge job with DuPont in Wilmington. Barry eventually married the telephone operator.

Jay Conner and I became good friends, played golf together at

Camp Shand, a small nine-hole course, and played on the Trickett softball team. I helped him and his wife, Janice and their infant daughter move three times during my second year. The first move was into a one-bedroom apartment with only light from the fire escape bedroom window. The second move was to the second floor of a three-floor apartment building with better lighting, but the third-floor tenants had to get to their apartment on third floor by walking through Conner's living room. Their third move and final resting place was on Pitt Street above the local house of ill repute.

Jay was very smart, never bought a book, took copious notes which he would transcribe every day after class and graduated fourth in our class. He retired as a judge in Delaware after being in private practice with me and others in DE.

I believe the forerunner to the modern drugstore was in Carlisle with the Swid Brothers, where one could buy anything cheap. We called them the Swindler Brothers. We were all poor, shopped at McCrory 5 &10, lived in less than plush surroundings, but we made do. However, Bob Papano, one of our classmates, lived in a plush apartment, as his father was a very prominent lawyer in West Chester and we and our wives were envious. We all drank a lot of cheap beer, had thirty-five-cent Manhattans at Clemson Party House once a month as members of Corpus Juris Society, a VERY VERY QUASI honor society. We consumed lots of hot dogs and beans, chicken livers and rice, salami and bologna sandwiches. We had kegs of beer for our parties and we all enjoyed our lives as poor "lawyers to become."

In the summer of 1962, I worked for a company called Capitol Products in Mechanicsburg, Penn., on the three-to-eleven shift, placing aluminum ingots into a rotary machine, which extruded window sashes, trim, etc. onto an asbestos table. My job was to guide the extruded material down the table some hundred feet and go back and start over again. Oftentimes extruded materials hit a rut on the table and all hell would break loose with a tangled mess of aluminum slivers all over the table. I wore a long-sleeved flannel shirt, asbestos gloves and a hat, and the plant was not airconditioned. I would get home at approximately midnight, very dirty and smelly, and had to take a bath and then spend time with my new bride, Connie. My boss, Harry Bowanoski, gave me only three days off.

We lived at 262 South Pitt Street on the first floor and there were two floors above our unit, with a fellow classmate on the second floor, but a tough-looking "hombre" on the third floor who clomped up the steps in the evening when he came home from wherever. Poor Connie, thrown right into the fray of being the wife of a law school student aspiring to graduate and become rich. Birds flew down our chimney, heat was fleeting and our furnished bed had a pronounced sag on the right side, where Mrs. Luckie, the prior tenant, must have slept, and she was immense. Her husband was in the military and weighed much less. Our landlady, Mrs. Shughart, gave us as a wedding present a repainted kitchen floor, with gray paint and white swirls. We had a VW Beetle, which I bought from my classmate Dave Bupp for a thousand dollars. After the monthly Corpus Juris meetings when I had drunk too much, I would run into the living room to check to see if the VW was there. Bad behavior and I never got stopped by the police, thank God. Our good friends, John and Nancy Bowman, lived on the first floor of an old apartment building next to the bus terminal and adjacent to the garbage incinerator, so our place was palatial compared to theirs.

Connie taught school to second graders in the local elementary school and made a small amount over four thousand dollars, which we used to survive in Carlisle, and we were happy as all of us were in the same boat. On January 5, 1963 – I believe the date is accurate – I was to take my first semester exams at Dickinson in my last year. While shaving that morning, I noticed stuff on my face which Connie knew was chickenpox. I had been Santa for her young students. Dr. Shaffer confirmed it upon my emergency appointment with him. I took my diagnosis to Professor Frankston and was permitted to take the exams a week or so later if I promised to not study further and not to talk with my classmates. I remember his stern warning, that as a lawyer I was obliged to act in an ethical manner, etc. I survived and evidently passed the exams, as well as the second semester exams, since I graduated in June 1963 and was twenty-fourth out of fifty-seven in my class, so in the upper half — a BIG DEAL. Graduating, for me, was a good accomplishment for an "Island Boy."

All in all, my legal education, both at Boston College and Dickinson, was rewarding, since I practiced law in Delaware from 1964 until 2012, had many clients with whom I became the friend of first and then their lawyer. A lawyer-client relationship has as its foundation the element of trust, which I believe existed with my clients in an office-type setting and which I spent my career in providing. Courtroom practice was not my style; office-oriented practice suited me better. I will devote an amount of space associated with my legal career in following chapters.

Wedding Day, June 30, 1962

Chapter 8
Young Parents and Dallam Road: Newark, Delaware, 1963-65

After graduating from law school, we came in mid-1963 to Newark, where Connie's folks lived. We moved into a small apartment attached to a larger building where Mr. and Mrs. Manning lived and operated a nursery school. Connie taught there. We had an infant daughter, Kristin, and a nice year or so at the "first home," with Audrey Ketner as a neighbor (her husband worked with Connie's father at the DuPont Company), frequent babysitter and companion for Connie. As budding home owners, Connie and I sanded the floors with an electric sander, did some painting, general cleanup and sprucing up, and made the dwelling very comfortable. One significant drawback was the sewage overflow which flooded our side yard periodically. No, we did not flush baby diapers down the toilet! I drove to work with H. Alfred Tarrant (Fred), a lawyer who lived down the street. I was clerking for the firm of Wise and Suddard and eventually joined the firm of Cooch and Taylor, where Fred practiced. He was instrumental in my hire. More on the Wise and Suddard experience later in this memoir.

Piet H. van Ogtrop

Chapter 9
Initial Home Ownership – 807 Kenyon Lane, Newark

A gentleman named Dick Prettyman, a realtor in Newark, who became a good friend for many years, was aware of our search for an affordable home in Newark, and in mid-1964 found for us 807 Kenyon Lane, a home with three bedrooms, a small living room, small dining room, smaller kitchen, two small bathrooms, no garage, a basement partially finished but with built in cabinetry, and a playroom. It was perfect for Connie, baby Kristin and me. We paid three thousand dollars and assumed a GI loan with a 4.5 percent interest rate. Monthly payments of principal and interest, taxes and insurance never exceeded ninety-eight dollars for our entire stay there. We were in heaven!

We quickly became suburban homeowners, created a vegetable garden, cut into closets and laid flooring in dormers for additional space, completely fenced in the rear yard (only three-fourths was fenced in when we moved in), religiously mowed the grass, kept flowerbeds neat, cleaned gutters, washed our Nash Rambler every weekend, dirty or not, weeded Mrs. Gilmore's property along our fence line, washed windows and storm windows, made bunk beds from two single beds (we hoped to have more children) and generally became the consummate young home owners. I painted the exterior of the home, made of stucco. Our neighbors were generally University of Delaware professors: Barwick, Cole, Matt, Kirch and other middle-class folk. The Miller boys (friends of our daughters), probably eight years old or so, threw mud balls at my neat house, which was not very neighborly.

We had no air conditioning but did have a window unit in our small bedroom, where the girls (Kristin, born in 1964; Valerie born in 1967; and Claire born in 1969) would come in and get into our beds to enjoy the cool air. We lived there from late 1964 until mid-1973 and the years there were wonderful.

The three other loves of my life: Kristin, Valerie and Claire, in the early 1970s

I remember experiences other than the ones just mentioned. We had a nice shed in our back yard which was the playhouse for the girls and their friends. One weekend we had a lot of rain and our back yard was flooded. Connie called me at the golf course to come home right away, as there were rats coming out from under the playhouse. Our neighbors behind us fed rabbits lettuce, tomatoes, etc., which evidently attracted the rats. I came home, got out my BB gun (where I got it I cannot remember), put on my wet-weather gear, and sat in my chair on the patio in the rain, firing shots a la Wyatt Earp. I was on a mission, which was eventually successful. I do not recall how many rats succumbed to my expert marksmanship.

A Boy From Aruba

Two more experiences I feel are worth noting and I vividly remember them after all these years.

We had a cocktail party in our little home and invited many more people than our home could accommodate, so it was packed. Fortuitously, it was a nice summer evening and the party spilled over into the back yard. We served Fishhouse Punch, a concoction of many different liquors, and made a HUGE bowl of it. Many people became intoxicated, wanted to dance, became loud and jovial and generally had a rip-roaring time. My two bosses at Cooch and Taylor attended and they both drank too much. One of our best friends, Frank Fierro, drank so much he had horrible headaches for days thereafter and his eyesight was actually compromised for a week or so. The *coup de grace* was that the glass punch bowl was empty and the glass dipper lay broken in the bowl when we were cleaning up in the morning. I guess the party was successful, as Frank Fierro still mentions it. Surprisingly, the neighbors did not complain.

Our daughter Claire was born July 6, 1969. Connie thought it okay for me to go play golf at the Newark Country Club, where we were members. Connie's Dad paid for our membership our first year. Well, it was going to be a great day, another child on the way, and I was two under par and putting for a birdie on the seventh hole. I had great expectations. Suddenly, Henry Dumont, a young French lad working in the pro shop, came racing down the hill to the seventh green, saying, "Mr. Piet, your wife called and her water broke and I do not know what that means but you need to go home." I knew what it meant and got home, but Connie had been taken to the hospital by our friend, Audrey Ketner. Lo and behold, daughter number three, Claire, entered the world, delivered by Dr. Hassler. I think I got to hospital AFTER the birth, so Connie's okay to let me play golf that day was not something I should have asked of her. I do not think I ended up in the doghouse and often wonder what score I might have had. I certainly did not raise the subject with Connie, or Claire once she became old enough to know what her dad did. I have made up for my transgression over time and all seems to be well.

The girls went to West Park elementary school and all in all, we had an enjoyable nine or so years at 807 Kenyon. For Kristin's memorable experience with the front storm door, I leave that to the reader to figure out or for Kristin to relate upon request.

Now, onto Chapter Ten and 110 Osage Lane, Newark, Delaware.

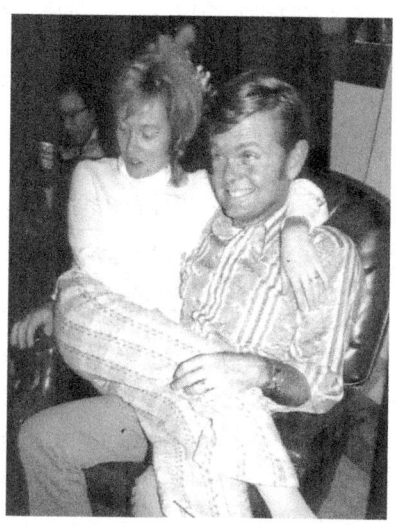

Drinking days: Piet with Connie

Additional drinking days

Chapter 10
The Joys of Owning a Fancy Home in the Country

Our home at 807 Kenyon Lane was becoming rather crowded with a third daughter, the need for each to have more space and their own bedroom and also for Connie and I to have a larger bedroom, more closet space, an attic and other amenities which my budding law career permitted us to afford. I knew an acquaintance in Newark who owned a lot in the development of Unami Trail, away from suburbia, per se, and which would be a perfect place to build a home.

We were forced to move out of 807 and had to live with Connie's folks with three children, as our new home at 110 Osage Lane being constructed and was not ready for occupancy.

The buyer of our home at 807 was a University of Delaware football coach. He and I had a verbal understanding that we could stay in 807 for a month or so until 110 Osage Lane was ready to occupy. The coach never advised his wife. She nixed our verbal deal and we had to move right after settlement. Bear in mind, I was a full-fledged lawyer by then and you would think I should have known better. Connie was very unhappy with me, understandably, and I ate humble pie for a long time but the saving grace was that we sold 807 for the unheard-of price of $33,900.

David Sysko and I struck a bargain and price and I had the property surveyed and found it larger than David thought by a factor of two. He did not renegotiate our bargain and we got a super deal. I had a client by the name of John Lester whose company built homes. Construction commenced and we were able to move in sometime in the late spring of 1974. Connie and I, along with help from our daughters (compatible with their ages), built flower beds; a terraced three-level garden with telephone poles we were able to beg, borrow and relocate; a vegetable garden; a quasi dog kennel under the deck; a basketball backboard and various and sundry other niceties.

Over time we converted the two-car garage into a family room with a woodburning stove and nice book cases and television cabinetry. The new room was a wonderful gathering place for us and very comfortable. A client and friend, John Muldoon, created a brick walkway and entryway which enhanced the aesthetic outlook of our home. John became a wonderful friend and more about him later.

Second house, Newark, Delaware

An unfinished basement became finished with the assistance of the Hart brothers and was a well-used room, adaptable for many uses. Connie's father helped me install two ceiling fans which we obtained from where I do not recall, and the installation was very tricky with cathedral ceilings. His experience as an engineer was invaluable and over time I learned a lot from him. There were a number of youngsters living in Unami Trail and the wait for them at the bus was always a scene. Kristin, as the oldest, went to Park Place, then McClary, then Shue and finally to St. Marks for four years; Valerie went to Holy Angels and then to St.

Marks for four years; and Claire, our youngest, went to Holy Angels, then to St. Marks for two years and to Newark High School for her final years. Forced busing became a very divisive issue in Delaware and we were not enthusiastic about our children being bussed into Wilmington to go to school.

Kristin, Valerie and Claire all participated in sports and so many trips to sporting venues were part of our lives at Unami Trail, with track meetings, diving meets, hot days sitting in the sun at Baynard Stadium, along with early morning trips for Val to a pool near the Delaware Memorial Bridge for her diving practice.

In her youth, Kristin was a high jumper, diver and swimmer, but now she devotes her energy to jogging, exercise and being a tough tennis player. Val in her youth was a swimmer and diver, with jogging now her main focus and voracious exercise with Cooper. Not to be outdone, Claire was a runner (still is), swimmer (never took a breath in a race), field hockey player with "Suse" in high school, and is now on the way to becoming quite an equestrian (she has two beautiful horses). They have a lot in common with the main focus being "workaholicism."

Connie and I painted the entire home at 110 Osage, a wooden home with wooden siding, and I wonder to this day how I avoided falling off of the ladder at the second floor level. Lots of snow, lots of shoveling and lots of tasks for all of us with mixed results. In lieu of ground cover around the perimeter of the home, yours truly used telephone poles, nicely cut, as borders, with MANY MANY loads of stone. On Thanksgiving Eve one year I severed the telephone line to our home while working outdoors in the evening on my landscaping project, which was not appreciated by Connie and the girls.

In one very embarrassing and painful experience, while reaching into the ice maker in the kitchen to get some ice, the lever moved forward and two of my my right hand fingers became stuck. I tried and tried to free them, while standing all the while on my tiptoes, without success. Valerie wanted to take an axe and demolish the apparatus and other attempts but she was dissuaded. So, Connie called 911 and between the time of her call and the arrival of fire trucks with horns blaring and police cars with lights flashing, someone, I do not recall who (although I believe it was Connie), unscrewed the apparatus and my fingers survived. To this day the tips off my fingers get very cold and numb in cold weather.

A client sold me an old VW for a very cheap price and it became the car for the girls. We named it Chitty Chitty Bang Bang for its frequent backfiring, acting up, stopping, starting intermittently, etc. and other ills. It spent a lot of time in the shop of a mechanic who assured me every time that the problems were fixed. On the day of Valerie's graduation from St. Marks, Chitty went on her final voyage. While waiting for Val to come from home to school for her graduation, we parents and Val's sisters were in the parking lot and Chitty, with Val at the wheel, made her final appearance, belching smoke, backfiring, shaking and rattling, and JUST STOPPED. Chitty, while legendary in the van Ogtrop house, went to the junkyard and so, sayonara to Chitty. We all laugh about her to this day.

Val did try once to see if Chitty could float as she tried to cross the creek and bridge on Hopkins Road after school during a flood one day, when it must have rained in record amounts. The bridge was crossed but Chitty and Val were both traumatized and perhaps that contributed to Chitty's demise.

In addition to selling Chitty to me for a cheap price, my client had a sister who lived in Augusta, Georgia and who had two tickets that she wanted me to have to the Masters Golf Tournament. I was not able to go on the days of the Masters, a regret I will always have, as walking on the hallowed grounds of the Masters is an experience that every golfer, whether proficient or a hacker, should have.

We all loved 110 Osage Lane and have many fond memories that we talk about when the subject of Newark is discussed.

A Boy From Aruba

Three of my four beauties: Claire, Valerie, Kristin

Piet H. van Ogtrop

Chapter 11
23 Mt. Airy Drive and West 11th Street

I am not certain of the dates and the appropriate sequencing but do know the essence of this chapter. One of the traditions we as a family undertook was to bring closure to our various properties and leaving 110 Osage Lane was no different. Kristin and Claire had done their thing in decision-making as to what they wanted from 110 Osage Lane, since we had an agreement of sale to sell it and move closer to Wilmington, as most of our friends lived in Wilmington. Valerie lived in California at that time and came East to say her farewell to the home she spent a large portion of her life in.

On the way to the Philadelphia Airport (the timeframe being pre-9/11), Connie was glancing through the newspaper and noted a property in Wilmington at 23 Mt. Airy for sale by owner. We had not made any decision as to a replacement property to purchase and were just looking to either buy or build. We stopped uninvited at 23 Mt. Airy. Patricia Johnson was very gracious and permitted us to take a quick look, and in discussion on the way to the airport, Valerie said, "That property is a non-contender," or language to that effect. We dropped Valerie off at her gate, bound for San Francisco, and drove back to Newark and 110 Osage Lane.

Feeling very morose about Val going back to San Francisco, we were about to take a walk. Our telephone rang. "Hi Piet, Bob returning Connie's call," and about which I knew nothing. Bob Stephenson was a good friend. After an exchange of pleasantries, Connie told Bob about our trip to 23 Mt. Airy and asked whether he had time to visit it with us. We had discussed some options, renovations, etc. on the trip home from the airport. Bob could not come until Tuesday sometime (we had taken Valerie to the airport on Sunday). I called Mrs. Johnson (Pat) about us coming back on Tuesday night. She advised that she already had an interested buyer who had not committed. A call back to Bob and a call to Pat resulted in Bob visiting the property on that Sunday night with us. Time was spent looking at it, thinking about what we could do to it, thinking about improvements, etc. We discussed it in the driveway and advised Mrs. Johnson that we wanted to buy the property.

The impetus for the hasty decision and our comfort for that haste was that Bob had done a major renovation to 110 Osage Lane and he wanted to build us another home in some manner. Bob had a son who was a good sidekick and could be part of a small crew. We had a deal with Rob, Bob's son, associated with our hire of him. We were under contract with Pat Johnson on Tuesday, three days after seeing the home.

Since we had sold 110 Osage Lane and had no place to go, we entered into a lease with Woodlawn Trustees to rent a row home at 2011 West 11th Street in Wilmington and therefore had a home to move into after selling 110 Osage Lane. The property at 23 Mt. Airy, while habitable and nice, was not what we really wanted as it stood. We knew that some major work to it was needed and we had to cover our bases with a place to live pending a move into 23 Mt. Airy.

Our stay on West 11th Street lasted about fifteen months and we were up to our eyeballs with furniture, etc., having moved from a four-bedroom home at 110 Osage Lane into a two-bedroom row home. The only eventful thing living ay West 11th Street was that the garage was packed to the gills with our things from Osage Lane which we could not get into the row home.

Bob, John Muldoon (a mason contractor and general contractor) and Bob's son Robbie became the three-man crew to rebuild a split-level home into a two-story beautiful stucco home. There were other people who worked on the project as needed, but I was the main grunt, tearing out walls, removing bath tubs, taking debris to the dump in Wilmington on 12th Street, and in general being very much involved. I hung drywall, sanded, painted, plastered, and so forth and "earned my stripes." Driving down 12th Street to the dump in John Muldoon's large pickup truck made me feel like Fred Sanford of Sanford and Son TV fame. I worked at the property after coming home from my daytime law job well into the night and spent most Saturdays and Sundays at the site.

After twelve or so months, the home was finished around Thanksgiving and we were ready to move in. The inspector who had to inspect the property was either sick or on vacation and would not give us a certificate of occupancy, as there was a change made to the design plan consisting of a retaining wall preventing flooding onto our driveway and street — a very sound and worthy idea. It had nothing to do with the integrity of the home at all. As the inspector was also not available and we had lots of things to move into the home, we just did it. I do not recall what the repercussions were but we did not go to jail, nor were we fined.

We had some twelve years at Mt. Airy and enjoyed our home very much. It was well built, had many amenities and served us very well. We did some major yard work, landscaping, hauling of copious amounts of mulch, removing shrubbery and trees and generally opened up our yard to more sunlight and air flow. We had a huge pine tree in the front yard which we donated to the City of Wilmington and it was set up in the main square in Wilmington at Christmas. We lived next to a state park with walking trails and we did a lot of hiking and snow shoeing with our grandchildren when they came to visit.

In 2012, I was obliged to retire from the firm of Morris James as they had a mandatory retirement policy when senior law firm partners attained the age of seventy-two, which I had. From early February 2012 until the fall of 2012, Connie and I cogitated as to what would be our plan moving forward. Our youngest daughter Claire lived in Pine Grove Mills, a suburb of State College, a nice place to retire, with her husband Gavin and three grandchildren. Greenwich, Connecticut and Pelham, New York, where our other daughters lived with their two and three children respectively, were too expensive in our planning. So, we put up our home for sale and had some interest from a buyer who gave the purchase some thought but did not feel ready to make such a large commitment. We listed the property with a realtor friend who sold our home at 110 Osage Lane and who did obtain a potential buyer.

The buyer had an inspection done and the inspector discovered a small amount of moisture in two obscure areas of the home. The buyer insisted upon the removal of ALL THE STUCCO. The property had been served by a cesspool for some fifty years without any problems whatsoever, as we had it pumped out every year and the company which pumped it out advised me it was unnecessary. However, the County officials would not grandfather our property and we needed a brand new septic system. Connie was recovering from breast cancer and had to recuperate with all the noise, dust and tumult while the necessary work was being done. All the stucco was removed by Zook Builders. That and the new septic system installed by Roser Company all amounted to some $70,000-plus. The buyer paid a very good price, so we swallowed the pain.

During the stucco remediation and new sewer line construction, I was on the golf course and Connie was resting when a gas company employee knocked on the front door and advised that they had ruptured a gas line to the property. How and why, I still have no clue. Fire trucks, police cars and HAZMAT personnel were all there when I came home from the golf course to a not very loving welcome from my bride! After all the hassle, the packing of our things, the visits from various charitable organizations for things we were not taking to Pennsylvania, we left Delaware and went to settlement on our home at 137 Brisbin Way in Boalsburg, Pennsylvania on July 15, 2013. More about Brisbin Way follows in Chapter 12.

Chapter 12
137 Brisbin Way, Springfield Commons, Boalsburg, Pennsylvania

Prior to the sale and settlement of our property at 23 Mt. Airy Drive, we made two trips up to State College, looking for a home we could move into in July of 2013, as we were not enthusiastic about making a double move to the area. We did find a home within the appropriate time parameters and made a deposit on it. Our daughter Claire, to whom we have been ever grateful, was aware of the fact that we really did not want the home with the deposit but just decided to buy it in resignation as we had made two unsuccessful trips looking for the dream house. Fortuitously, the seller wished us to give her a much larger deposit so she did not sign the contract.

In the interim Claire found out that 137 Brisbin was for sale, in our price range, in a very desirable area next to woods, with little traffic, and other amenities. "Mom and Dad, you need to come up one more time. I have found the perfect home for you," she told us. We were not overly anxious to make an additional four-hour trip but decided to do so. It was on a Sunday afternoon. We checked out the house, told the realtor we wanted to buy it and as it would be vacant on July 15, it was perfect. The realtor prepared the paperwork and we were under contract on Monday morning. The previous contract was withdrawn, the deposit was returned, and everything was "hunky dinky," as my father was known to say.

The settlement up here in PA went very smoothly, the papers were signed and the funds from the sale of 23 Mt. Airy were wired to the local PA settlement office. We were able to coordinate the move from DE to PA without any difficulty and it was splendid. My sister Marca was a HUGE help to us with cleaning, packing and organizing, both the move out of 23 Mt. Airy and the move into 137 Brisbin. The whole experience was a lesson in great organizational skills demonstrated by Connie and Marca, and I was just the grunt doing some heavy lifting.

The home suited us perfectly: a three-bedroom, two-bath, two-story home with a two-car garage. It had a large crawl space, a nice front, side and back yard and a vacant lot next door where our grandsons could play soccer, and when at "Grammy Camp," could play on some large dirt piles down the hill, as the development was new and only partially built out. We often sat out on our back deck and enjoyed the quietude and the view of Mt. Nittany across the valley. We were in bear country and periodically Mamma Bear visited our neighbors, Alan and Katie, and their two-year-old. It wasn't a fifty-five-and-over community and Alan and Katie became surrogate children and we were very fond of them. Connie created a beautiful butterfly garden in the back yard, the envy of the neighbors, and we enjoyed gardening.

I became active in our Homeowners Association and spearheaded some actions against some persons in our Association who were troublemakers. I served on the Association's Board of Directors and enjoyed my ability to provide useful service, which benefitted our community. The overwhelming majority of the people living in the Springfield Commons Association were genuine and neighborly. The association today is vibrant and the community is very much flourishing, and we keep in touch with our friends we made there. We were fortunate to sell our home to a very nice lady and are pleased the transaction went as smoothly when we sold the property as when we bought it.

Our plan in the waning years of our lives was to not be a burden on our children to care for us. Connie was a major caregiver for her mother who had dementia while we lived in DE and she also took care of her father's needs when necessary after he moved into a retirement home in DE for some number of years. Thus, when I became eighty-two we decided to move into a retirement facility known as Foxdale. We moved here in January 2021. We had been on the waiting list for some years.

Our journey with regard to housing will end with our residency in Foxdale and some discussion relative to that is in Chapter 13.

Chapter 13
Residency at Foxdale as an "Inmate"

Connie's father spent his final years in a retirement facility in Delaware on the fifth floor and then the ground floor in a very nice facility called Cokesbury, and he characterized himself and others as "inmates." Connie and I moved into a very nice facility some four miles from our prior home, called Foxdale, and we hardly consider ourselves as inmates. We have a nice apartment with two bedrooms, a den for Connie to do her painting, a large kitchen, a small living-dining area and two bathrooms. It fits our needs perfectly. We have a patio that we can enjoy with room for some furniture and it gives us ample space to enjoy the outdoors. Our unit has a lawn and a large enough series of flower beds and Connie has spruced them up nicely. We are the youngest in our neighborhood, known as the J neighborhood, with neighbors in their late-eighties and early-to-mid-nineties, and our neighbor John Homan is now aged one hundred. He was a B-24 bomber pilot at age nineteen in WW2, flew thirty-five missions over Germany and still has all his marbles! A remarkable group of people that has welcomed us with open arms and we feel very fortunate to have such nice new friends.

We both keep busy with various committees, social events, lectures and social gatherings of all neighborhoods A-L inclusive (there are some three hundred-plus people who live at Foxdale). We eat some of the meals here and cook in maybe four times per week in the large kitchen. The food is not bad and for seven dollars for a dinner, a bargain. Connie and I have become good friends with two other couples who are not Foxdalers, but are Connie's bridge partners, and the six of us go out to dinner on Friday nights. All in all, a very good move for us and we are happy living here, although we miss the yard and openness of our previous home. I cannot believe that I almost neglected to mention the GREAT HELP our three daughters were in our move from Brisbin Way and into Foxdale. They unpacked boxes, put dishes, pots, pans and all sorts of items in proper places and we were essentially moved in the day we moved out of Brisbin – beds made, furniture arranged and total control taken over the project. We indeed are very fortunate with our three wonderful, talented, energetic and loving daughters.

The practice of law occupied some forty-eight years of my life, with various and sundry episodes along the legal pathway, which I will refer to in the following chapter, broken down into separate "stops."

Chapter 14
My Legal Career from Inception to Closure

Permit me to state that I had a very rewarding legal career, primarily from creating new relationships of trust, understanding and meaningful assistance. I perceived the practice of law as a service for which I was compensated. My philosophy was quite simple – my first task was to gain clients as friends who had confidence in me and secondly, once I gained their trust, then I would become their adviser for which I was paid. I was not a court lawyer, I did not try cases, I was not a litigator and my practice was office and transaction-related – residential and commercial real estate, wills, trusts, estate settlement and estate planning, and in my final ten or so years, elder law. I was blessed with many clients in my years of practice and I believe they felt I treated them with the respect and courtesy they deserved and the legal advice they expected. The following relationships and associations permitted me in my legal career to have pursued the desired goals.

Upon completion of law school I was able to obtain a deferment from induction into military service until after the bar exam. As best as I can recall the dates, my deferment ran out in July 1963. Two days prior to my reporting date in Cleveland, Ohio for a pre-induction physical, Connie found out she was pregnant with our daughter, Kristin. Back in those times, fathers and/or expectant fathers were exempt. Notices were sent to my draft board by telegram (no faxes, FedEx or other swift communication) and I did not have to report. I would not have had to go to Vietnam, as this was well prior to our country's involvement there, but the possibility could have existed. I would have been a "buck" private and would not have relished the idea of doing KP duty for minor infractions, which really would not have impacted my ability to serve. I absolutely would have served my country and but for the miracle of childbirth, was deprived of that privilege!

Piet H. van Ogtrop

WISE AND SUDDARD

I mentioned earlier in this memoir H. Alfred Tarrant (Fred), who was very instrumental in forming my career. Fred lived down the street from Connie and me and I drove into Wilmington with him while I worked at Wise and Suddard and he, Fred, at Cooch and Taylor. After graduating from law school in June, 1963, I was to take the Delaware bar exam soon after, in July, but had to complete a six-month clerkship with a DE law firm before being admitted to the DE bar.

Wise and Suddard interviewed me and evidently thought I was worthy to clerk for them. Henry Wise was a brilliant man for whom the practice of law was a second passion. He was married to a Mellon heir, had a large yacht and money was no object. Oliver Suddard was a very interesting man, quirky, full of himself, foppish and somewhat of a dandy. Richard Allen Paul was a young lawyer some four years older than I and very competent. I did legal research, attended perfunctory hearings for both Messrs. Wise and Suddard, and was a "gofer." I did not believe it was necessary for me to study for the bar exam, there being a hiatus of only a month or so between completion of law school and the exam.

The bar exam consisted of a grilling on Saturday morning before the written portion of the exam, with some thirty or so essay questions. The grilling dealt with my being questioned on a roughly-seven-hundred-page book, titled "Zane's History of the Law," and the grillers were Henry Canby, Richard Corroon and James McKinstry. Mr. Corroon was a pillar of the bar and asked some inane questions which I was able to answer with Jim McKinstry's intervention. So, I passed the condition precedent to taking the written portion of the exam and felt confident that the written portion was a piece of cake. Alas, I FLUNKED the bar exam, as I was deficient in the Civil Procedure questions, and Jim McKinstry, my mentor for the exam, advised that a bar aspirant had to pass all of the written portions. Well, Wise and

Suddard had no further use for my services and I parted company with them in early September 1963.

Fred Tarrant mentioned to his colleagues at Cooch and Taylor that I could fill an open position it needed to fill, namely in doing what young lawyers did back then, searching titles. Fred and Cooch and Taylor came to my rescue, for which I was very grateful. I did a good piece of work for Henry Wise in writing his brief for an exploding Coca Cola bottle case he argued and won in the Delaware Supreme Court, but that was evidently not enough for me to be retained by their firm. My departure may have been a blessing in disguise, as Oliver Suddard was horribly injured in a glider accident some few years thereafter and did not return to the practice of law.

COOCH AND TAYLOR

Upon joining Cooch and Taylor, I was put to work searching titles, as Donald Taylor and Edward Cooch, principals, along with young associates, did real estate work, both residential and commercial. While the work was not overly challenging, it did provide for me an avenue to explore once I passed the bar exam, for which I DID STUDY in Cooch and Taylor's offices in the Wilmington Savings Society building after working hours and on the weekends. Cooch and Taylor had an office in Newark and as I lived in Newark, it became a good fit for me to have a presence in Newark after I passed the bar.

I was admitted in December 1964 and I received a bonus of one hundred dollars, which was a large sum then. The firm also had its main office in Wilmington and I had an office there. I spent considerable time learning the many facets of Wills and Estate planning from Robert Crowe, who was a contemporary of mine. I knew my focus was to be an office-oriented practice; real estate and estate planning, estate settlement, wills and trusts and related issues became my practice of choice.

I do recall my first venture in the practice of law. Mr. Cooch asked me to review a matter for him and communicate my analysis to William Prickett, a senior member and bar icon. Very proud of my analysis and feeling confident of my ability to persuade others of my legal abilities, I sent a three page letter to Mr. Prickett in which I respectfully requested his response. It came this way. "Dear Mr. van Ogtrop. The answer is NO!" My bubble burst but I overcame the jarring defeat.

COOCH and TAYLOR

ATTORNEYS-AT-LAW

ARE PLEASED TO ANNOUNCE THAT

PIET H. VAN OGTROP

HAS BECOME ASSOCIATED WITH THEM

IN THE GENERAL PRACTICE OF LAW

EDWARD W. COOCH, JR.
DONALD C. TAYLOR

601 BANK OF DELAWARE BUILDING
WILMINGTON, DELAWARE

H. ALFRED TARRANT, JR.
PIET H. VAN OGTROP

WILMINGTON SAVINGS FUND SOCIETY BUILDING
NEWARK, DELAWARE

DECEMBER 10, 1964

Beginning of law career in Wilmington, Delaware

The firm had young associates, younger than me, who did not work particularly hard, nor did they actively seek to cultivate their own practices. I spent many hours in the office on the weekends and after the official closing of the office at five p.m., while the young associates treated their association as a nine-to-five job only five days per week without working on Saturdays and Sundays. They received their paychecks and there were many times when the senior members of the firm (I was among that group) had to wait for their pay, as times were sometimes difficult. As a young lawyer with three children, I counted on a regular paycheck and it galled me to see younger lawyers in the firm not having to wait like I had to.

I spoke to Donald Taylor, a senior partner, about this on many occasions, and he and I commiserated about the situation, but nothing concrete was done, as Don was a senior bar member and financially much better off than me. I did not let my dismay or angst affect my performance, but the situation took a drastic turn of events for me in the spring of 1976.

My law school classmate, Jay Conner, was in practice with Robert Daley and James Erisman with an office in both Wilmington and Newark. Jay had approached me many times about joining his firm and I did not wish to do so due to loyalty to Donald Taylor, security, loyalty to Fred Tarrant and "principle." Jay and Janice came to our home for dinner on a Friday night in March 1976 and after some drinks and banter, he said to me, "Piet, I will not ask again, this is my final offer. I want you to join Bob, Jim and me and we will pay you ten thousand more than you are making now. Let's drive down to 206 Delaware Avenue and we can see what you will be involved with."

Cooch and Taylor had not had a particularly good month and I had not yet received the balance of my February pay. With that in mind, I told Jay I would accept with a caveat that I needed to speak with Don Taylor to advise him of what I was proposing to do. First thing Monday morning, after much soul searching, angst, sweat and fear, I approached Don in this office. I recall it was before eight in the morning and no one else was in yet. I closed the door and in a halting and stammering manner (I remember it very well to this day), I explained to Don what Jay proposed. Don, being the consummate gentleman that he was, answered me after my presentation, "Piet, if you believe this is good for you and your family, who am I to say no." I broke down in tears and he and I hugged and I left his office. I called Jay at his office and called Connie and the deal was done.

I had a great deal of work to clean up at Cooch and Taylor, and while it was emotionally draining, I left the firm on June 1,

1976 and took up residence at 206 E. Delaware Avenue as a member of a new firm, which even had my name on its letterhead. The move was also difficult because my brother Bernard was at Cooch and Taylor and I wanted him to know that I was not abandoning a sinking ship. My friendships with Fred Tarrant, Bob Crowe, Donald Taylor, Edward Cooch and other lawyers, secretaries and staff at Cooch and Taylor remained in good standing and that indeed was gratifying.

CONNER, DALEY, ERISMAN AND VAN OGTROP (to change over time to Daley, Erisman and van Ogtrop, and finally to Erisman and van Ogtrop)

Walking into 206 E. Delaware on June 1, 1976 was an uplifting and gratifying experience. I had a new-found interest in working more diligently, as there was no senior member of the bar to fall back on and I needed to show my new colleagues that they did not make a wrong choice in having me join their firm. I had a secretary from Cooch and Taylor join me, Jeanne Downes, a very good secretary, spunky and a self-starter. I also was very fortunate to have Mildred Frazer (Millie) agree to join me as a real estate secretary. Both Jeanne and Millie had worked with me at Cooch and Taylor and did secretarial work for me.

The office was an old brick dwelling. Upstairs was a small office and conference room, and downstairs, a small conference room, a small office, a supply closet and room for two secretaries. The waiting room was in the hall leading to upstairs. For my entire time at 206 E. Delaware Avenue, from 1976 until 2008, the only change made was to have a new roof and an interior paint job. There were two very large sycamore trees in the front yard and they created a mess when shedding their leaves and bark.

My daughters were my cleaning crew and they also did some yard work, albeit that it consisted of weeding and some minor cosmetic work as there was no yard to speak of. I do not recall ever washing the windows. There was an old white fence that was eventually taken down and the driveway and parking pad were eventually asphalted. The red carpet was never removed and central air was not considered as two window units sufficed.

As I had spent a great deal of time in Cooch and Taylor's Newark office, I had acquired a following with clients in wills, trusts, estate settlement and real estate. Vance Funk, a good friend, and I had a small corner of the real estate market and we became friendly competitors. On the day Vance had a stroke, I had met with him earlier in the day on some matter and he did not seem right. I called his office and spoke with one of his secretaries and told her to check up on him. He had a stroke in the late afternoon on the trunk of his car and Sheila, his secretary, was aware and was very instrumental in getting assistance. Vance survived but became partially disabled and he expressed his gratitude to me often.

The firm was "loose" in that we all just went about our business without a lot of rules and protocols. We met periodically in the Wilmington office and the lawyers in that office, Jay Conner, Bob Daley and Jim Erisman, would come to Newark periodically for appointments and to just visit. The relationships among the four of us were very good and solid and although we had all four names on our letterhead, we all did our "thing." We did have a partnership agreement and an operating agreement but did not delve into each other's affairs. I was generally the Newark office partner and responsible for it, and the Wilmington men were responsible for Wilmington.

We each leased cars and the firm paid for the lease payments. I had a very modest car and the Wilmington men had fancy cars. As I was responsible for "all things Newark," I saw no reason to have a fancy car. We had the books of the firm prepared by a book keeper, Al Hammett, and he just wrote down numbers and we did not need any real advice. Eventually we engaged a female person who was more professional and she kept us straight.

The car lease situation may have triggered an audit by the IRS and we once met with an IRS auditor, Jack Brodsky, in our Wilmington office. Jack came into the conference room loaded for bear, pulled out all his paperwork and began his inquiries. Jay

Piet H. van Ogtrop

Conner had a pair of Phillies-Dodger baseball game tickets in his pocket which must have piqued Jack's interest, as he exclaimed to all of us and told Jay, "I am a Dodger fan." Jay being ever vigilant, countered, "Here, you can have these tickets." Books and papers were closed, audit was completed and we were happy and the IRS also, MAYBE. We were never bothered by the IRS again.

We had raucous Christmas parties for the entire staff, lawyers and spouses and one in particular stands out. We held our party at the Mendenhall Inn, a swanky and popular place with patrons whose decorum was better than ours, and at least for one night we all behaved so loudly and badly that we were asked to leave and we never again were permitted to use the Inn for any CDEVO event. Alcohol flowed freely and singing was absurdly loud, so it should not have come as a surprise.

We had a fishing trip every summer out of Bowers Beach, DE and invited real estate persons who had sent us business. There was a copious amount of fried chicken, a lot of beer and many contests. We would leave Bowers about two p.m. and return to the docks at eight or so, sunburned, smelly, slightly drunk and greasy from the chicken.

The captain of the boat, Dave Davidson, provided all the fishing poles, nets and other paraphernalia associated with being fisherman. I had never fished in my life and on my first outing with my new firm, I was prepared to "catch the big one." I did not only catch nothing but in my casting of the fishing line, I let go of the entire reel, line, etc. and it remains at the bottom of the Delaware Bay. My little mishap cost me some ninety-five dollars. I had to pay it from the Newark office checkbook but could not write it off as an expense! On all subsequent trips I drank beer and ate chicken and left the fishing to the professionals.

Jay became a Family Court judge, I believe, in 1988, and the firm changed its name to Daley, Erisman and van Ogtrop. Jay was a very good lawyer and a "rainmaker." His parting from the firm changed our philosophy and although we were named DEVO, we essentially became sole practitioners. I was solely responsible for Newark and Bob and Jim were responsible for Wilmington. Bob died in the mid 1990s and Jim and I then became Erisman and van Ogtrop. We both had good practices and could each carry our own load with the responsibility for the respective offices.

There was a short period of time when Bruce Hudson, a very competent lawyer, was part of the firm but that did not last very long. Additionally, the four of us, Jay, Bob, Jim and I, were approached by Cooch and Taylor (the firm I had left) about joining forces but that did not materialize as there were philosophical differences between us and them.

I had a short association with a lovely young lawyer, Michele Muldoon, for approximately one year. I was concerned about my ethical responsibility to my clients to make certain that their affairs would be attended to upon my retirement, which was on my radar. Michele, as a young practitioner, did not feel qualified or financially able to carry on and our relationship ended. Her parents were clients of mine and her dad and I would see each other at WAWA in Hockessin every morning at six-thirty on our way to our respective jobs, and have some coffee. The fact that Michele and I did not continue our association was a significant factor in my joining Morris James, an iconic firm in Delaware, to complete my legal career.

My association with Jay, Bob and Jim was very rewarding and I grew as an attorney in both attitude and experience. I was blessed to have a number of long-standing clients and I feel I served them well. My career at CDEVO, then DEVO, then EVO, gave me the confidence to practice essentially as a solo practitioner. I enjoyed the association with Jay, Bob and Jim and my decision to join them certainly was vindicated and a decision that I never regretted.

Jay, Bob and Jim owned the property in Newark and Wilmington and I "bought in" when I joined them. Over time we were very fortunate to buy out Jay's interest when he became a judge, and also Bob's share after his death. Jim and I ended up vacating the property at 1224 King Street and were very fortunate to sell it to a fellow lawyer in Wilmington who graciously agreed to up the ante by ten thousand dollars so that we would not have to pony up monies to sell. We had refinanced the property to buy out Jay and Bob's widow and all was well. Jim and I were sole practitioners with his maintaining an office in Wilmington and I joined Morris James.

MORRIS JAMES

One of the ethical obligations which are binding upon all lawyers, whether in sole or a group practice, is the responsibility to preserve and protect client files and affairs. Being essentially a sole practitioner in Newark after Jim and I had our own separate practices, I was very concerned with how my clients' affairs and documents would be protected and their affairs taken care of upon my eventual retirement. I was over sixty-five and the issue of retirement was on my radar.

James Semple, Esquire, a friend of mine from the workout room at Wilmington Country Club, knew that I was very concerned with the issue and as I had a good and successful practice, suggested that perhaps I would consider speaking with Morris James about joining it. Without a great deal of negotiating (Morris James was very generous and professional, as is its well-known reputation), I joined Morris James on June 1, 2006. Morris James removed all of my files from my Newark office at 206 East Delaware Avenue and calibrated all the files of some forty-plus years of practice into their system. We had sold the property at 206 E. Delaware Avenue to a lawyer colleague, Bruce Hubbard, some months before and so the move to Morris James at 116 Polly Drummond Hill Road in Newark was a painless process. I had a new office, a new colleague (Kevin Healy), and new secretaries in the office who were very pleasant and helpful. I brought my secretary, Valerie Dangel with me to Polly Drummond Hill Road. My tenure with Morris James ended January 31, 2012 when I was obliged to retire consistent with the firm policy that lawyers attaining the age of seventy-two were obliged to retire. I was actually seventy-two in February 2011 but they gave me some latitude. As a *quid pro quo* for not extending my retirement past that, I agreed to relinquish my law license to practice in DE, as the firm perhaps (?) was concerned that I would continue to practice in Newark and that perhaps I would "hang out my own shingle" in Newark, as I still enjoyed my practice. At risk of braggadocio, I had a good reputation, many clients and still enjoyed going to my office. The resolution of my leaving the firm was mutually satisfactory.

Morris James, being a very large firm with diverse specialties and four offices, was eye-opening in discovering how a large firm operates. My stay with the firm for the five-plus years was a very valuable and exciting experience and I believe I provided value to it. I made new friends and acquaintances, and am forever grateful to Morris James and its attorneys and staff that my clients' well-being and affairs were protected after my retirement.

All in all, my legal career was a source of pride for me and in general I enjoyed going to my office and I never lacked for work. I enjoyed my clients and they brought me satisfaction in my career.

Piet H. van Ogtrop

Chapter 15
Various Sports

As a young man, I fancied myself a reasonable athlete and played baseball, softball, bowling, golf and an occasional game of tennis. My main focus post-college days was on golf, subsequently tennis, and then skiing. An Aruban does not ski as there is no snow and no mountains, but despite that, I did end up starting to ski in my late thirties with the prodding of my friend Jay Conner and loved the sport. Although I never attained any semblance of being able to ski the "blacks" expert trails, I did become reasonably proficient with the "blues" intermediate trails. I am devoting this chapter to the three sports I enjoyed the most in my twenties and thirties and still enjoy in my later years. I'll start with golf. The golf memories are many and enjoyable to reminisce about.

GOLF (in Aruba and post-Aruba)

My first exposure to golf was at Aruba Golf Club, a nine-hole golf course built for Exxon employees. Mr. Charles Garber, a friend of my parents, gave me some of his old clubs when I was thirteen years of age. The course was built out in the wilds where grass was hard to grow and coral was abundant. The course had two sets of tees to make it an eighteen-hole course. There was a semblance of a driving range where I hit balls often. The greens were oiled sand greens, and being the last player to complete his/her putt was no fun as the bottom of the hole would have an oily residue.

I often caddied for Mr. Garber and my compensation would be new golf balls. I became reasonably proficient and purchased a set of Hogan clubs from Bill Burbage, a golfer much older than me, for one hundred and fifty guilders, an absolute steal. On Saturdays shortly after noon, the golfers who were employees descended on the course to play, and although I was too young to play with them, I remember them fondly. Messrs. Fuller, Binetti, Adams, Taylor, Branham, Radell, Leak and Garber are among the players who come to mind. The gang played their eighteen holes and then sat at the bar and drank their Heineken beers and tallied their scores and wins/losses. My golf mates were some classmates, older and younger than I was, Terry Richey (a good girl golfer), Jerry Barnes, Richard Beers, Bob Burkhard, among others. My brother Bernard will no doubt remember the large series of bushes on the left side of the ninth hole. Well, in my junior year I had a three-shot lead on the field and had the ninth hole to play. I hooked my shot in the bushes, had a score of nine and lost my high school championship to Richard Beers by one stroke. I still think "what if."

I played on my college golf team as the sixth man my sophomore, junior and senior years in college, but never became better, as putting on manicured grass greens was my undoing, having putted on sand greens all my young life. After college my golfing days were numbered, as studying in law school was a priority. I did play with my friend Jay Conner at Camp Shand in Carlisle, a rinky-dink course by normal standards but fun nevertheless. Once in a while we would venture out to play Cumberland Valley, a course built on farm land, where green fees were twenty-five dollars for eighteen holes.

Connie's father gave us a Christmas present in 1965 of a membership at Newark Country Club. I played there often and have fond memories of a large group I used to play with every Saturday – Pinto, Deck, Richitelli, Dingle, Murray, Smith, Tuttle, Hooper, Statler and the Hart brothers, among others. We always had at least twelve players and sometimes I won some money and sometimes I lost. My first significant client was R. Doyle McSpadden, a local businessman, who introduced himself to me the first day I set foot on Newark CC. Doyle, Sam Keim, Sank Richards and I played a lot together and they were much older than me but we became true friends until they all passed away. Newark CC was a place for me to get my feet wet. I was a member at Newark CC from 1965 until 1981, when I "went

A Boy From Aruba

uptown" and joined Wilmington Country Club, the creme de la creme of Delaware golf, with high rollers, landed gentry and other socially-connected folks.

An enjoyable event which I was invited to was an annual trip to golf courses in North Carolina with fellow Newark golfers, Bob Hooper, David George, Dr. Berger, E.C. Hewlett and a lot of golfers from York, Pennsylvania. The first year I was invited, the Newark golfers drove down in their own cars as did the York gang. The following year the whole group of us rented a bus and had refreshments on the way down, along with many laughs. For five days we had the bus at our disposal, with the driver, and that made trips to Pinehurst, Southern Pines, Pine Needles and Foxfire duck soup.

Foxfire had a retired military man, a man named Donovan, who was a pain in our behinds and made us feel very unwelcome. He and Bob Hooper almost duked it out. A lot of poker playing, plenty of drinking and late nights. The course records remained intact but we tried hard. A dentist from York, Sam Jajic, showed the Southern gals how Northern men behave when challenged. Sam was in a group in front of four Southern belles who were not happy they could not tee off ahead of his group of four. Sam rifled his first ball into the water, causing the girls to murmur. He did it a second time and the murmur became more pronounced, and after ball three went into the drink, the gals really became very annoyed and had loud collective sighs. Sam had a retort: "If I hear any more from any of you, I will throw your Southern a...s in the drink." All of us Northerners laughed and laughed and Sam made our day. Sam was a lousy golfer! The trips were great fun and Bob Hooper and I became lifelong friends, to this day.

I had some interaction with Wilmington Country Club members before joining, as there was a group organized by Michael Walsh, a career re-elected New Castle County Sheriff. We would go to NJ, PA and DE to play various and sundry courses. Being part of the Walsh group made my initiation to Wilmington Country Club much easier and I fit in without too much difficulty. My first outing at Wilmington was with Bill

Wolhar, among others, and walking up to the eighteenth hole we discussed what our wives were involved with. Bill's wife was a cancer survivor and Connie had written her thesis on cancer related issues. The girls spent three hours on the telephone that night, and Bill and Becky, Bill's wife, became good friends with whom we played a lot of golf and socialized, until Becky passed from cancer and Bill moved to Florida.

Among highlights of my golfing days at WCC was membership in the Wilkie group, where some sixteen of us would travel to various venues to play golf. It was an enjoyable and congenial group and invitation to membership was coveted, although I did not consider it that special. Membership in my later years in the 9–19ers was the grand finale to my golfing days at Wilmington. The club was formed to insure that anyone seeking a game could join after a cursory vetting process and would be assured a golf date on Saturdays starting at 9:19 a.m. The club had grown to forty-five members when I left WCC and I have many fond memories. The group was very sexist and I am not aware of any changes to that outdated policy.

My golfing days at WCC would not be complete without mentioning with great fondness my outings on Tuesday afternoons with Whitey (P. Gerald White) and Blackie (James Blackwell). We would play eighteen holes, have lots of laughs and banter, take our showers and then meet in the grill for dinner. I believe we did this for at least ten years and I very much looked forward to being with them, as they were among two of my best friends.

Tom and Judy Barone established a Sunday afternoon mixed-golf outing at WCC with dinner and prizes to follow. We generally had some sixteen or so participants and it was a fun afternoon. Connie participated with some other women with whom she played during the week. She initially was a nine-holer but became proficient enough to be invited to the eighteen-hole group and played in some inter-club events. Her game was very respectable, although she and I both suffer from putting woes.

I resigned from WCC when we moved to Pennsylvania in

2013 and joined Centre Hills Country Club in Boalsburg, PA. I made new friends at Centre Hills and played on Tuesday and Thursday with two groups. When we moved to Foxdale in 2021, we resigned from Centre Hills and now have a minimal membership at Mountain View. Jerry and Pat Gearhart were golfing friends with whom we played at Centre Hills and who now live at Foxdale and also belong to Mountain View. Jerry and Pat are in their mid-nineties and still play golf very well. Once Connie and I recuperate from some aches and pains, we hope to play a lot of golf in our waning years and we'd enjoy playing with Pat and Jerry. Connie did play with a ladies group at Centre Hills but a rotor cuff issue, which has since been repaired with a new shoulder, prevented her from playing as much as she would have liked.

Arnie and me, 2020

Piet H. van Ogtrop

I am not sure where my relationship with Jay and Janice Conner fits in, as we have had many ski stories which I will relate in my ski memories and adventures, but golf experiences were many. Jay, Janice, Connie and I used to take a vacation day to frequent many of the local golf courses in DE, PA and NJ on Thursdays but never in the Wilmington area, as Jay and I were supposed to be at work. We had many outings, both in warm and cold weather. One course near Wilmington was Brantwood in Elkton, MD and its fifth hole was across the street from Baker's Restaurant and liquor store. We would stop there in cold weather for a peppermint schnapps to keep warm. After golf we ate at Baker's, where chicken and dumplings with dark meat cost a dollar sixty-five and Manhattans seventy-five cents. We often imbibed too much but were never apprehended by the constabulary.

Jay was a member at Rehoboth Country Club and he invited me to play with him as a partner a number of times in Member-Guest events. We usually won a prize and had good times. On Friday nights, as reciprocation by me and Connie, we picked up the tab for our journey across Rehoboth Bay to enjoy dinner and drinks at Martini's, a local restaurant.

One particular year we went over to Martini's in Jay's boat and Jay encouraged us to remember the compass settings for the return trip to Rehoboth. After a fun evening of abundant drinking and eating, we returned to Rehoboth trying to recall the compass settings. Unfortunately, on the way back to Rehoboth, in a semi-intoxicated state, we ran aground on a big sand bar in the middle of Rehoboth Bay at midnight or so. We were unsuccessful staying in the boat so the four of us stripped down to our undies, etc. and after much pulling, pushing and laughing, we were able to become freed from the sand bar. We returned to Rehoboth at approximately two in the morning and to celebrate our success we had a night cap at a local bar, whose air-conditioning was tough on the girls. We got to bed at around three and had to be up at seven for an eight a.m. tee time. I recall that we did win a prize.

Jay and I thought our golf games would get better if we had new clubs and so we began the process of making our own, ordering heads for clubs, shafts, grips, etc. I think we each made four sets and became reasonably proficient. Jay made a forty-eight-inch putter which was later outlawed by the golfing Gods. On one memorable day the four of us went on one of our midweek junkets and Jay had just finished making a new driver earlier the previous weekend. Well into the round, having used his new driver at least twice, he used it a third time, and having had no trouble with it before, he took a mighty swing and the head of the driver went further than the ball. Fortunately, the head went down the fairway and not behind him, so none of us were in danger of being injured. We laughed and laughed and laughed, and Janice, who always had a good sense of humor, coined Jay as "Basement Bob" since he did his club assembly in his basement. We still laugh about it to this day. Golfing with the Conners was always a lot of fun.

SKI VACATIONS AND EXPERIENCES

I closed the golf section with experiences with Jay and Janice Conner, and so it is only fitting that I open the ski portion of this chapter by again invoking fond memories with the Conners, who introduced us to the sport of skiing. Neither Connie nor I had ever skied – we were complete novices. Jay had started to ski at a very tiny ski area called Chadd's Peak so his sons could learn how to ski.

I do not know how much skiing Jay had done before one Friday in February, 1977, when he came to the office in Newark with his Spider Sabich ski sweater on, and red tight ski pants. The secretaries were very amused (they really liked Jay for his mischievous ways) and had no idea. Well, he had set up a ski trip to Mt. Snow in Vermont with Dr. Bruce Smith and wife, Dr. Jerry Zippelli and wife, himself and Janice, and wanted Connie and me to be the fourth couple. Jay and Janice have twins sons, Mark and

Todd, who were ten years old or so. All four couples went to Mt. Snow in Vermont for a week in March 1977. Connie and I were outfitted with skis, boots, poles and all the other paraphernalia and ready to conquer the mountain. We had an instructor, Tommy Goodman, who suggested 135cm skis for me. The first day on the skis, on the beginner trail, doing whirly birds and other non-skiing moves, my short skis did not prevent me from crashing into plastic netting at the bottom of an almost flat trail and I sprained both of my thumbs.

I eventually was put into longer skis by Tommy with some semblance of success but not much. I was the only male in a group of eight skiers, seven secretaries from Washington, D.C. and me. One of the secretaries was very funny but scared to death when Tommy announced we were all going to ski down "the Beaver," an almost flat trail. "Oh no, not the Beaver," she exclaimed. The Conners and I still get a laugh out of that remark. At the end of the week, Tommy suggested I either quit skiing or get more liability insurance.

The Conner boys were as mischievous as their father. One night at dinner they counted the number of times Bruce Smith said, "yeah, right" in his conversation. The boys counted seventy-six times! We still laugh about that. Our first venture at skiing with Jay and Janice turned into many wonderful ski trips with plenty of laughs and fun.

The Conners provided the impetus to engage in various ski adventures and there were many places we skied, both with friends and also with family. I will simply mention some memorable ones. We went to Austria in the mid-eighties with our three daughters and skied at Lech and St. Anton. Magnificent terrain and vistas and we all loved our trip, although we were all beginner skiers and the vast terrain was somewhat overwhelming.

On our trip back to the U.S. we boarded a train in Zurich, having driven there from Austria for a visit with some distant relatives of Connie's. We were on our way to Brussels for our plane trip back to America. We had all our luggage, ski bags, and other stuff with us and were settled down for the long trip to

Brussels. I heard on the intercom that the car where we had our skis stored was uncoupling and going to Hamburg and so, in the nick of time, we rescued our skis from that car and we made it safely to Brussels. Upon arrival in Brussels, we were made aware that our flight time was moved up and we were successful in hitching a ride with a van driver who agreed to take us to the airport for a very reasonable fee. We made it to airport some fifteen minutes before our flight and had we not made that flight, the next flight to U.S. was two days later. The snow Gods were watching over us as this was pre 9/11.

Ski bunnies

Piet H. van Ogtrop

We had many ski trips with our children to Park City, Utah, where we purchased a time share at a distressed sale for $4,400. The vO, Hooper and Hess families spent many fun times there and our girls became quite proficient skiers. We did take all three girls, their children and our sons-in-law in 2010 for a family vacation. Our condo paid for itself many times over and we felt it a good investment.

Family photo with grandchildren, Park City, Utah, 2010

The Hoopers purchased a ski condominium at Greek Peak in Marathon, New York and again, the vO, Hooper and Hess families spent enjoyable times there, sometimes with children and often just the three couples. Bob Hooper became friendly with an apple orchard owner and introduced us to Mitsu apples, which were good eating as well as for baking. Trips to the Virgil firehall for pancake breakfasts on Saturday was also indulged in once or twice with the entire three families, and Karen Hooper's boyfriend at one occasion ate some twenty pancakes. The mountain was fun and very skiable and we felt that our skiing had progressed so that we could handle the blue trails with aplomb.

The ski trips with the Conners were too many to mention, but again, one stands out. Bob Daley had a client who owned a condo at Camelback in the Poconos and Jay and Janice, Bob and Helen Daley and Connie and I had our annual three-day trip there. Chinese food was always on the menu and Jay mistakenly ate five or six ultra hot peppers and suffered abundantly. We never forgot that trip. Often it rained on our trip and Daley, being an Irishman, was coined Mr. Murphy — if things can go wrong they will. Daley was often bad luck and we skied in the rain with garbage bags on over our ski clothes.

There was a small group, spearheaded by Jay, who went to Poconos to ski on Thursdays. We always stopped on the way home for a six-pack of beer and a bag of potato chips. In later years, we skied at Little Gap (later called Blue Mountain) near Allentown, PA and instead of beer and chips, we stopped at Longacre's for delicious ice cream.

Jay planned trips to Sugarbush in VT, Sugarloaf in Maine, Waterville Valley in VT, and various other spots in the New England states. One trip with eight couples to Cranmore, Pico, Killington and Bromley was also memorable. Four ladies took turns cooking the dinners. One evening Bonnie White was the cook and prepared a sumptuous dinner and Janice Conner was responsible for some portion thereof. After a long day of skiing in the brisk and sunny New England cold, Janice spent time in the hot tub, drank a beer and followed that up with a strong Manhattan, which she enjoyed. The dinner bell rang and Janice was nowhere to be found. After a search of our respective bedrooms Janice was found, face down, fast asleep or otherwise, on the floor between the beds in their unit. She never lived it down.

Art DiSabatino, a friend of all of us, planned a trip to Utah where eight couples skied at Park City and Park West and then at Alta and Snowbird. We were delighted as a group that Art made the arrangements, as it took a lot of time and effort. Little did we know that he put all the expenses on his credit card and benefitted by having many frequent flier miles in his account. He was a judge in DE and Jay and I chided him often for his lack of candor, which the judicial canons of ethics compel him to adhere to. Art was also a tennis buddy so it was all in jest.

Connie and I had a blank wall in the lower unit of our home on Mt. Airy Drive and I decided to decorate that wall with trail maps of all the various places that Connie, the girls, grandkids, friends and I had skied. For many of the places I already had trail maps and for others I had to contact the ski areas. I had all the maps laminated and thumb-tacked them on the blank wall, arranged by states. I counted them one day and to my surprise I found that we had skied over fifty places, when skiing did not cost an arm or a leg as it does now. The maps served as placemats for messy grandchildren when they would come for dinner and some of them still are with us. I think we skied all the ski areas in New England other than Jay Peak. We never went to Canada but also skied areas in N.Y. Does the reader know where Belleayre is?

I have to add to this section the vO trip to Camelback in the Poconos in Don Boyer's travel trailer. He let us use it for a weekend trip. The drive up to Camelback went fine with no mishaps. The debacle began on Friday night. The heat went out in the trailer and we all froze that night. We decided to drive back to DE on Saturday rather than endure another cold sleepless night and drove after a full day of skiing, with diminishing headlights as the battery was going bad, no heat, the trailer was leaking some fluid, what kind I did not know, and we limped into Don's driveway and thanked him but never used the trailer again. Connie and the girls were unhappy campers.

The last comment on skiing. Being an over-solicitous father regarding the welfare of my daughters, I panicked one time in Park City when my girls went up into Scott Bowl, an expert area which only the ultra-good skiers could ski. I did not know where they were until Connie told me and I told Connie they were in deadly peril and I prayed they would make it down alive. Not only did they make it down alive, they did not fall and they laughed at me for my "deadly peril" concerns.

My girls will remember the unfortunate trip to Villa Vosilla in N.Y. at Hunter Mountain. Claire, as a very young child, had a bad day as she became very sick from the food at Villa Vosilla or the dirty sheets and general unsanitary conditions.

With the exception of isolated events, our skiing experiences were wonderful and a significant part of our lives were spent in that sport. Jay Conner was very instrumental in our skiing career and we reminisce about his teaching us how to make S-turns and various skiing maneuvers. The vOs and Conners have many fond memories of skiing but alas, with the ravages of time and some physical issues, we have all hung up our skis.

Our dear friend, Janice Conner, wife and companion of her husband, Jay, became a "character" in the lives of me and Connie beginning in 1962 and the fun times we had with Janice and Jay are too numerous to mention. Janice fought a very courageous fight with pancreatic cancer and passed away in early September 2023. As her name appears frequently in this memoir, I did not think it inappropriate to give her some special recognition. There are no moguls, three putts, etc. in heaven, Mrs. Basement Bob.

TENNIS

The fact that tennis occupies the third position in my sporting life and experiences does not minimize its importance and enjoyment in my life as I consider my tennis experiences to be entitled to equal time.

I played tennis in Aruba in high school and recall that I was the high school champion my senior year by beating Jim Stoveken. It was not a big deal as there were only two of us in the tournament. After my high school tennis I did not play again until the late 1970s when Connie and I played social tennis in Newark with Bill and Judy Vaughn.

Upon joining Wilmington Country Club, I was invited to join

a group with Art DiSabatino, Jerry White, Jim Blackwell, Henry Tatnall, Dick Deery and my brother Bernard, among others. We played on Tuesday night, both outdoors and indoors in the winter, and after tennis, we ate dinner in the men's grill. The tradition lasted some twenty-five or so years until we disbanded due to deaths, physical problems, and other reasons. I was generally paired with Jerry White and we became very good friends and played social tennis with Jerry and his wife Bonnie very often. We also played paddle tennis in the winter which was a new experience but similarly enjoyable.

My interest in tennis really mushroomed when we moved to PA in 2013. I was very fortunate to have been invited to play in Tom Smith's Sunrise group, which played twice a week, both indoors and outdoors, and the group consisted of some twenty or so players, male and female, and still exists today. There are various levels of ability but notwithstanding that, we are a very close-knit and enjoyable group. The clay courts at Penn State are very good conditioned courts, as are the indoor Har-Tru composition courts. Tom Smith is our "Commissioner" and creates the pairings for our various times and dates and our group has become one in which tennis players desire to be affiliated. We played at seven thirty in the morning and in later years at nine. Tom's group has been and continues to be a good source of exercise and friendship. The group expanded to four days, beginning at nine until ten thirty and the group members are both sexes with all levels of play. It is a very competitive group.

Connie has not played tennis since leaving DE because of shoulder issues but was a loyal and enthusiastic player at WCC and hopefully will be able to again play here in PA when her body permits.

Chapter 16
Vacations and Various Trips

At the risk of being braggadocio, but with an abundance of good fortune, savings and good planning, Connie, the girls and I enjoyed many trips and vacations, as well as trips with just her and me, and trips with the girls, sons-in-law and grandchildren. In previous chapters I have discussed some trips of ours which we considered memorable: skiing in Austria, many ski trips in the U.S. and other vacations.

One of our favorite places to vacation is a YMCA vacation on Sandy Island in the middle of Lake Winnipesaukee in New Hampshire. Connie and I started going there in 1969 with two of our daughters, who were then seven and five. Claire was an infant and my mother babysat her in Washington, D.C. We have made many friends over the years who come from a variety of places and while things have changed for all of us, a visit to Sandy is always a trip we look forward to. Our initial visit has morphed into attendance by my siblings and their children and grandchildren. One year, of the one hundred and eighty-two campers, some seventy-seven had some connection to van Ogtrops — everywhere you went on the island, some van Ogtrop was around. Sadly, with grandchildren now having their own schedules and parents having different priorities, the visits to Sandy are probably on their last legs. So, no visits to the outhouse in the middle of the night, spiders, raccoons, lack of air-conditioning, bathing in the lake with bio-degradable soap, abundant fattening food, line dancing with the little guys ... all were part of making Sandy a good family vacation.

We have a family reunion on the Maryland shore with some of my siblings at a cottage owned by my nephews and that is also an enjoyable weekend. My mother and father used to come and enjoyed being with their children and grandchildren. One of my sisters became friendly with a Catholic priest and he said Mass at Scientists' Cliffs (the cottage) and their platonic relationship ended in his being released from his vows and he married my sister. Joe was a special man and over time my parents became very fond of him. He died of a massive heart attack some seven years ago as of the date of this writing, and we think and speak of him fondly.

We celebrated Connie's sixtieth birthday at Outer Banks in N.C. with all our girls, sons-in-law and grandchildren, which almost was cancelled after three days of tremendous rain storms, and playing Uno, Monopoly, checkers and cards was becoming boring.

We had the good fortune to go on a trip to Ireland with one of our daughters, her husband and our three grandsons. It was a great trip and Ireland is a lovely country. We also took a trip to Alaska with another daughter, her husband and two grandsons, which was also not only memorable but very exciting with rafting through schools of seals, watching Orcas fighting, etc. Trips with our daughters, their spouses and our grandchildren have been a wonderful experience for us all.

As we celebrated our sixtieth wedding anniversary on June 30, 2022, I do not think it presumptuous to also mention trips by Connie and me to the Canary Islands, Algonquin State Park in Canada, Costa Rica, Hawaii, Italy, New Zealand and Australia (for our fortieth), Italy, Iceland, Prague to Berlin (an OLLI trip), Canadian Rockies (Road Scholar trip), Holland, Austria and California. Dividing the sum of sixty years of wedded bliss by number of trips over time, I do not think we overdid it. This memoir may come into possession by others than our girls and grandchildren, and so we hope you will indulge me in suggesting we are spending our girls' inheritance before we go up to the "Pearly Gates."

Connie, me, our three daughters, two of our sons-in-law and all our grandchildren went to Aruba some fourteen years ago to celebrate my seventieth birthday. It was a trip down memory lane and very nostalgic except for the fact I could not find my old high school and the community where I was brought up was totally changed. A humorous event which could have had bad repercussions took place, and but for the grace of God I might not be telling this episode.

Our unit in the complex looked like all other units and ours and our daughter Valerie's was on second floor. After my workout at the gym, I went to what I believed to be Valerie's unit, where we usually all "camped out." I looked around, thought it looked like our unit with some changes Valerie must have made over night. I went to the refrigerator, drank some juice, ate a bagel, read a magazine and went out to porch. Two units over Valerie and Connie called over, "Dad, what are you doing there, that is not our unit!" I had advised the cleaning person that cleaning was not necessary as we were leaving the next day. I immediately left the wrong unit and went to ours. Thank goodness no females, young or old, exited any rooms or bathrooms, with or without clothing, to confront the trespasser, as Aruba law is very strict with regard to anything that has remote sexual or other bad behavior. I would have been arrested and life would have been hellish moving forward, with all kind of bad endings. I never did find out who owned the unit I invaded nor did I hear from anyone in management and thank goodness the cleaning lady knew nothing was awry.

All other vacations went smoothly without any mishaps or surprises.

Piet H. van Ogtrop

Chapter 17
Friends

Connie and I were blessed with wonderful friends wherever we lived and a small chapter needs to be devoted to them. While we lived in Newark, we had good friends in our Newark gourmet group, Panaccione: Graziano, Rudy and van Ogtrop, all of whom lived in Unami Trail. Subsequent to that group, a later group formed with Ries, McMullen, Hammond, Scott, Smith, and van Ogtrop. The latter group was together for well over ten years until death of some members caused the group to shrink and eventually disband. One of my closest and best friends is Bob Hooper, and our friendship commenced in 1964 and continues to this day. Bob and his wife Carolyn were skiers and fellow golfers and we had many good times. I have already mentioned Jay and Janice Conner as particularly good friends.

Even though we lived in Newark, the majority of our friends were from Wilmington with friendships created from Wilmington Country Club members: Wolhar, Barone, Jerry and Bonnie White, 9–19ers, John and Nancy Bowman, law school friends, and many others. All friends are special for all of us but certain ones stand out.

Since moving to State College, we are one of the "Three Muskateer" couples. Connie was befriended by Marilyn Furry and Irene Harpster through Bridge and the three couples have made it a habit to go out for dinner every Friday night and also go on trips together. When we moved from Springfield Commons in Boalsburg to Foxdale Village, we left with heavy hearts as we made some good friendships and thankfully we can see them periodically as Foxdale is not far away from there.

Tennis, bridge, golf and painting have become avenues to cultivate new friendships here in State College. I have been fortunate to be a member of the Tom Smith tennis group and have made some warm friendships with both the male and female members. Connie has joined a bridge group here at Foxdale and also a painting class, where she is continuing to hone her skills.

Lastly, we are the youngsters on the first floor of our apartment building on the J floor and have made some good friends. Every Friday at four-thirty we have, for the J floor residents, a gathering where all subjects are fair game and it is euphemistically referred to as an "attitude adjustment" by John Homan, our discussion leader.

I believe that, in our waning years, good friends are precious gifts. If this memoir might see the light of day with those who were my friends in grade school, high school, college, law school and my life to date, thank you for your friendship. I will always treasure it.

Chapter 18
Miscellany, Random Reminiscences, Various and Sundry Experiences and Good, Bad and Questionable Behavior, Not in Any Sequence or in Chronological Order but as I Recollect Them

I went to school in Aruba from kindergarten through twelfth grade and while I received a D-minus in physics, a very daring and foolish venture was engaged in by me and Billy Johnson. As discussed in Chapter 1, there were foolish pranks and/or behavior. Billy and I dyed our hair green for St. Patrick's Day in our senior year and were suspended from school for three days. I was also suspended for a day for putting my feet up on the desk in Miss Gallicani's Spanish class and three days by Miss Mills for announcing in Math class that she shaved her arms and getting close to her was "strange."

Billy Johnson and I were ring leaders with mischief in Aruba. I spent one night in jail during my senior year in high school for a very stupid prank. Cars back in the 1950s had their horn engaged by depressing a rod-like apparatus coming out of the steering column. Johnson and I thought it would be cool to tie down some thirty horns at the movie house. Well, Officer Mono (Spanish for monkey) was driving around, saw us and took us to the "pokey" where we spent the night, with no comforts, and we were not read our Miranda rights! We had to reimburse the folks whose cars were effected. Butch Hudson, Warren Norcom and Larry Riggs were also involved but got away.

In college, Sam Vitale and I, with names near the end of the alphabet, wanted to take a popular course which was a requirement in our majors, but the class was filling up very rapidly. We doctored up some of the paperwork but got caught, and not only did we not take the course until our senior year, supposedly after a year of resting on our laurels, but we were suspended from school for one week for behavior unbecoming a Jesuit schooled student. Father Schell, the President of John

Carroll, told Sam and me that if we did not get into any further trouble, our records would be clean. It is hard to get too drunk on 3.2 percent beer. As I was from Aruba, I had no place to go, and Clem Tully, who lived in Cleveland, permitted me to "bunk down" at his parents' home for the week. Sam was from Chicago and went home. We both survived and did not disclose our caper on any important post college documents and our records remain clean.

As a young associate at Cooch and Taylor, I, along with the others in the firm, were invited to a big cocktail party at Don Taylor's home. Well, I drank too much and spent most of the night in the bathroom, which would generally have been used by all the guests. Dorcas Taylor, Don's wife, not realizing that I drank too much, opined, "Poor Piet, he must have eaten something which did not agree with him." Connie and I had driven to the party with Fred and Shirley Tarrant in their Ford convertible. I did not make it quick enough with rolling down the back window and became very sick in the well of the car. Shirley was very kind, thought I had a stomach bug, but Fred knew better. I cleaned the car the following day and it took a long time for me to become a partner.

I came to the United States with a green card (I was not a citizen yet) and had an international driver's license. Connie and I went to a fancy cocktail party in Philadelphia, where I again drank too much, and I always insisted on driving. For those of you familiar with Route 1 and Route 202, it is a major intersection. I decided go take a left from the extreme right hand lane of Route 1 (not a left hand turn lane).

On our merry way back to Delaware, a flashing red light came into view in my rear view mirror, and being a law-abiding citizen, I pulled over to the side of the road. Officer McGruff approached the car, "License and registration. Whose car is this?" "My father in law's." Looking at my green card and international driver's license, he exclaimed, "What the hell are these?" Sobering up immediately, I explained Connie was my wife, I was at Dickinson Law School, I was not yet a citizen, and all other exculpatory info.

He exclaimed, "Ma'am, you get behind the wheel and Sir, you get in the passenger's side. Get the hell out of here and don't let me ever see you again." I was very lucky and laws in 1962 were more relaxed than today. I also was not arrested, so did not have to report my bad behavior to Dickinson Law or the Delaware Bar Association. The trooper was very courteous and kind and as it was in the Christmas season, an early Christmas present!

One day after Thanksgiving when we lived in Wilmington, I had the bright idea to clean the gutters on my porch. The porch had frost, the ladder slipped, I landed on my elbow and broke it. Connie took me to the hospital in Wilmington where I underwent elbow surgery by the doctor, a golfing buddy, who was called from the golf course to do the surgery. No more ladder, as Connie took it to the curb to be left for the garbage, a wife who had to wait until late in the evening before we went home, and a disappointed golfer who was on his way to shooting his best score ever, so he told me. Alas and alack.

Between my junior and senior year in high school, I had a summer job working for a company called Chicago Bridge & Iron, which built large oil tanks to store the oil processed in the refinery. Once the tanks were emptied and the oil shipped to various spots in the world, the tanks needed to be cleaned and readied for subsequent use. My job consisted of scraping the tank interior, sweeping up residue and debris and getting the tank ready for a new delivery. I had to wear a long-sleeved shirt, long pants, a mask, a hat, goggles and other protective gear. At the end of the summer, I had to stay in the hospital covered with a black salve designed to extract debris which permeated my skin. I recall I was in the hospital for some ten days. Saving grace – I was well paid.

I did not have a Social Security card when I came to the U.S. and obtained one in Cleveland shortly after I entered college. My only identification at the time was a green card, as I was considered to be a non-resident immigrant. My name on the card had my first name as Piet, which is my correct first name. Ms. "Cranky," a bureaucrat, told me she was not familiar with that name and issued my Social Security card to Pete Van Ogtrop. All of my official paper work has either Pete or Piet. When I applied for my Social Security benefits some twenty years ago in DE, they scoured my records for a Piet and did not find one but did find a Pete. I had to sign an affidavit that Pete and Piet are one and the same. So, my Social Security, Medicare and other government papers are in the name of Pete, but when I was naturalized in 1962 in Carlisle, PA, the naturalization papers show me as Piet. Government at its finest!

My law office in Newark was a haven for bats who decided to make the attic their home and the second floor walls a place to "hang out" both literally and figuratively. I do not know how they got there, but perhaps when the interior of the office was painted the painters left the doors open. The little creatures did no harm and thankfully no clients or secretaries were affected. There were frequent trips from the exterminator to 206 East Delaware Ave. and they finally were totally eradicated.

On my way with my buddies to dinner at the Theta Chi house while in second year of law school, we had to walk past a female dormitory. One winter evening my buddies and I had a contest to see who could throw a snowball upon the roof of a five-story dormitory. I had a pretty good arm from playing baseball in my earlier days and I came the closest, but unfortunately my snowball broke a window and sitting at the window was the sister of one of my law school classmates. I knew who she was and after making contact with her in the lobby of the dormitory, found out she had glass in her hair, in her undergarments and all over her desk. She was not injured and after much apologizing and offering of help, I was relieved and went to dinner at the Theta Chi house. Today I would be served with papers and sued for millions! Again, I was very lucky.

As a seventh grader in Aruba, we had an outdoor movie house where all the movies were shown under the stars. The reader may remember an actor by the name of Boris Karloff, who starred in the movie "Frankenstein." Well, I went to the movies by myself and sat through Frankenstein and was petrified. I called home to

A Boy From Aruba

ask my folks to pick me up but no one answered the phone so I ran all the way home. Unfortunately I made a mess in my underwear, and I now know where the phrase "scared the shit out of me" comes from.

My wife Connie has made many trips to various hospitals for me: broken hand, broken elbow, MRSA and other mishaps. She has advised me that she will no longer take care of me so I have to resort to non-breakable mishaps. I had a PSA checked in DE in 2012 and it was close to four and the doctor told me to keep an eye on it. Upon moving to PA in 2013, the protocol for men over seventy (which I was) was that PSA tests were not necessary, or so goes the scuttlebutt. Entering Foxdale in 2021, I had my PSA checked at the insistence of Dr. Sepich, the doctor at Foxdale to whom I am eternally grateful, and found my PSA was 126. His reaction was, "Wow, this is highest I have seen" and "you definitely have prostate cancer but will not die from it." I am being well taken care of with a sophisticated regime of injections and hormone treatments to prevent cancer from spreading. This is a peculiar matter to place in a memoir, but if any males read this and are over fifty, GET YOUR PSA CHECKED!! Connie is very supportive and helps me along the path of doing exercises, etc. to return to a degree of pre-cancer living.

This reminiscence is actually quite funny and as an American who can still speak and understand Dutch, perhaps the reader will enjoy this incident. When I lived in Aruba, I played sports and would frequently come home hot, sticky and sweaty. My folks had a friend, Fern Garber, who would stop down for a cocktail with my folks before our supper.

I always engaged my folks and Fern in small talk and on one occasion asked my mother when we would have supper. She gave me the info and I responded, "Well, I have time to take a douche." A shower in Dutch is a *douche*. Fern had a drink up to her lips and burst out laughing and sputtering and could not stop. I am surprised she did not choke. Anyway, I get a lot of mileage out of that little ditty and knowing some Dutch can go a long way.

An American of Dutch heritage cannot properly pronounce the name of the airport in Amsterdam. It is *Schiphol* and Americans have a hard time with the gutturals. I am taking some liberties in suggesting that I am tri-lingual, as I know enough Dutch to get by and being an Aruban, know Papiamento, a mix of English and Spanish with a little Dutch mixed in.

Chapter 19 follows as the last chapter of the third stage of my journey through life, and although I believe that I may be past the middle of stage three, I hope to have many more years to enjoy life's experiences. As I write this, while I do have prostate cancer, I'm receiving excellent care and treatment and anticipate that my number will not be up for some time, as I hope to shoot my age in golf before going "upstairs."

Chapter 19
Dedicated to My Family and Their Importance to Me in My Various Stages of Life

Chapter 19 is saved for last in this memoir, as it relates to the most important persons who have helped form my life — my mom and dad; my siblings; my wife Connie; my three daughters, Kristin (59) Valerie (56) and Claire (54); my sons-in law Dean, Cooper and Gavin; and my seven grandsons and one beautiful granddaughter.

My father graduated in 1935 from the University of Amsterdam medical school with his focus in urology. He practiced in Holland a short time and then in early 1938 was offered a position in Lago Colony Hospital operated by Esso in the Urology Department. He signed a three-year contract. Things in Europe were not safe; with the situation in Europe deteriorating and the threat of war being more than just a threat but an actual reality, my parents left Holland in May 1938, bound for a short stint in Aruba. They hoped to acquire a little bit of a nest egg which would help them enter the working world back in Holland with their families. WWII fully entered the picture and my parents were "stuck" in Aruba, for which we seven children are eternally grateful. My folks left parents and siblings behind when they left Holland and I am sure this caused them some remorse, but they never expressed that to me. I know that my aunts and uncles were affected by WWII and we in Aruba were not impacted. I have many cousins and relatives in Holland whom I have never met and I was not really a "Dutchie."

My dad was one of seven children and my parents had no qualms in following suit as I am one of seven siblings. As the eldest, I was born in 1939, brother John in 1940 (fifteen months later) and every two years thereafter another van Ogtrop kid appeared. Maria (Muff) in 1942, Bernard (Dick) in 1944, Marca (Martha) in 1946, Elsje (Elizabeth) in 1948 and Patricia in 1950. My parents were strict Catholics and the infamous rhythm method used by Catholics did not work for them.

One of my sisters passed away in November 2022, having succumbed to inoperable brain cancer, which afflicted her for some five years. Otherwise, we children of John and Martha have had a charmed life. Seven is a lucky number!

Our lives in Aruba, as seven of the van Ogtrop "clan" as we were known, was a life enjoyed with abundant sunshine, fun, lack of being saddled with problems of the other parts of the world, and generally a very cloistered existence. We received a good education in the American established school system (I had to take the infamous New York regents to matriculate in the U.S.). We were as American as any of our friends.

John Bernard van Ogtrop (28) and Martha Elmyre Povel (27) were joined in matrimony on May 3, 1938 in Bussum, Holland. Two young marrieds, probably not knowing a lot of English or Americana, took a huge leap of faith when they embarked upon their trip into the unknown by going to Aruba, a tiny island in the Netherlands Antilles, nineteen miles long, six miles wide, inhabited by goats, donkeys, iguanas, beautiful beaches, constant sun, warm days and pleasant nights and general euphoria.

Martha Povel, when she was dating John van Ogtrop

A Boy From Aruba

Martha and John in Holland, before they married

Esso, now Exxon, had a very large oil refinery that processed aviation fuel (oil came from Venezuela on flat-bottomed oil tankers). The refinery, as facts would later confirm, played a very significant role in air warfare in the Battle of Britain and Allied successes in WWII. I was three years old in 1942 when German U-boats shelled the refinery and sank shipping. I remember being taken by my parents, along with younger brother John, to the hospital high on a hill overlooking the refinery.

Upon arriving in Aruba mid-May 1938, they moved into bungalow 315 of company housing provided for foreign staff employees: Americans, Dutch, English and other non-Arubans. My dad went to work at Lago Hospital seven days after arriving in Aruba, leaving his new bride to become used to the new surroundings. They acclimated well; they built gardens and a swimming pool with brickwork and cemented walls, but with no way for water to be recycled, so the pool was constantly being filled with fresh water.

My parents were fortunate in that a number of the hospital's doctors and support personnel were also Dutch – Schenstock, Ruyter, DeGoede, Schelforst and others, to name a few. My parents became part of a Dutch community while becoming acclimated to American style. The hospital was very large and had some fifty doctors, as it served the entire population of Aruba – some sixty thousand people. My dad was a urologist whose expertise was in demand, as the mode of travel around the refinery was on motor scooters with much "jostling" and kidney issues.

Brother John and I were born in bungalow 315. My folks outgrew bungalow 315 and moved into bungalow 484, a bigger home, where Maria, Bernard and Marca were born. We lived in bungalow 484 until the early 1950s or so and then moved to bungalow 32, right on the Caribbean Sea with the shore a stone's throw from our home. Dad and I would go across the lagoon in a small boat with a five-horsepower motor to a sandy bar to pick up flotsam from which my dad built a dock, complete with a shed, wooden steps and a landing. My dad was a very good carpenter and he built the area along the lagoon, with a wooden chaise lounge, tables, chairs and other "toys." I was not aware how talented he was.

Piet "helping" his dad build the bath house in Aruba

A Boy From Aruba

Rogues' gallery: brothers John, Piet and Dick

I do not recollect how our times were spent, but we did a lot of swimming and nautical things and a favorite treat was swimming on Christmas Day to ward off the spiked eggnog we all drank too much of. We had a beautiful garden, a comfortable patio, a fish pond and swing set. My folks were very good to us and wanted to be sure there was plenty for us to do. It was when we lived in bungalow 32 that my Dad bought a small English used MG auto from one of his colleagues. He loved his little toy and it was the only semi-extravagant thing I recall my dad indulged in for himself.

From bungalow 32, my folks downsized to bungalow 74, with only Elizabeth and Patricia at home, as the others were away in college in the U.S. I am not sure of the dates, happenings, etc. as I was older than my siblings and had established a firm footing in the States. I do know that all of the stays in various bungalows had their share of happy experiences for all of us, parents and children.

Piet H. van Ogtrop

An idyllic spot: our house at the center

Another shot of our last house in Aruba. Note Dad's MG.

A Boy From Aruba

My folks left Aruba in 1968 and went to live in Clarksville, VA with my youngest sister, Pat. It was not a pleasant experience and they eventually moved to Rockville, MD to be closer to MD children and DE children. My dad "retired" in 1968, prompted by a decision Exxon made that a non-American should not become the medical director of a large American hospital in an Exxon facility. My dad was unanimously chosen by his colleagues but Exxon had final say, and so Dad's medical career was too short for his liking as he loved being a doctor and care giver. Upon moving to Maryland, when he was only fifty-eight years old, he explored practicing in MD with a large hospital. The bureaucratic nonsense and the sum of $25,000 to qualify in MD was the last straw. Dad permanently retired, much to his dismay, with a blow he had a difficult time reconciling to as his skills were not questioned.

Dutch pioneering parents
John and Martha, Rockville, Maryland

Piet H. van Ogtrop

Aruba was a good period in my parents' lives. Dad was a very respected doctor whose patients had a great feeling for him. He was Dr. WON OCTRUP – the people could not pronounce his name, but we were known as Dr. WON OCTRUP's children. We children wore that badge with honor while my folks were alive and continue to be proud of our heritage.

My dad was modest, self-effacing, kind, generous, religious, and loved our mom and his children, and reveled in their successes. I am not sure how he and my mom swung seven college expenses as I did not recollect my parents having independent wealth. They made do and were obviously good at it. As my folks had seven children, there was not a lot of one-one interaction between parent and child, but none of us were ever neglected and both parents were very instrumental in starting us on a good path in life. My parents were both religious and taught us the importance of adherence to the Ten Commandments. There were periodic "slip-ups," but nothing which would have been an embarrassment to our folks.

I believe, and this is pure surmisal on my part (although our deceased sister Marca, as family "historian," would have known) that my dad's grandfather, and in turn my dad's father, may have had an interest through "inheritance" in a Dutch gin business, titled Winand Focking, which was famous for its ultra-strong Dutch gin, called "Genever." I make it a practice to not fool around with the name of the company when talking about my father's career with my American friends. I may be totally wrong with this surmisal but it might make sense.

My mother was a "rock" and really had the family under control. Having given birth to seven children, she was a tough gal. Just over five feet tall, maybe one hundred pounds and full of p--s and vinegar, she also had an ornery streak which made her lovable and unique. Hooting and hollering at kids' sporting events, pulling out family pictures of her children for anyone interested, sales at the commissary (we had no grocery stores self-standing and bought our stuff at the company commissary) were legendary. Forty-eight cans of Dinty Moore stew, Spaghetti-Os,

Spam (how we hated that) and various and sundry bargains, she would turns into tasty meals. She would go out to the village (St. Nicholas) and buy seven pairs of Keds, seven of various items of clothing and always looked for bargains. She was a great partner and companion for my dad. In her waning years, she developed Alzheimer's and my dad was her caregiver for many years, clearly evidence of this love for her and his "gift" to her for the load she undertook taking care of the needs of seven kids.

I would use the following words to describe my parents and I think my siblings would agree. The references are not their sole characteristics, but the most memorable ones.

MY MOM – Funny, irreverent, always pregnant and not euphoric about it, good cook, good organizer, proud to be my dad's wife, very religious but not repugnantly so and in general a wonderful wife and mother. My mom enjoyed creme de menthe after a nice Sunday meal, given to her by Dad, and we seven kids would hoot and holler, "another kid coming in nine months." Mom did use her pregnancies and subsequent births as fodder for her bragging rights about her family. She was one-quarter French, one-quarter Italian, one-quarter English and one-quarter Dutch. Once when I was in high school, I came home and got into a discussion about France's role in WWII and Vichy France. After my lambasting of the French, my mother, having not said word one during my diatribe, stopped me in my tracks. "Don't forget, *snot neus* (smartass in Dutch slang) that I am part French." You could have heard a pin drop.

MY DAD – Very modest, unassuming, very generous, very proud to be a doctor and help the disadvantaged, religious, extraordinarily devoted to my Mom with her Alzheimer's (she had it for close to ten years), very interested in children's sporting events, always had a little speech at family gatherings, which often times "drug on" too long. My dad was a complicated man who played his cards close to his vest. I do not recall him ever disparaging anyone and he rarely displayed a temper, although he would have had occasions to do so. He sat at his radio every night listening to Dow Jones results and also stayed up late to listen to

Dodgers games. My folks never became U.S. citizens and my dad's reason was very simple: "Eisenhower is the only one I would vote for and he is not running!"

I described my father as a modest man, but I, along with many others, remember him as a man devoted to helping others. He was employed by Exxon and devoted many hours to his corporate responsibility. There was a hospital in Oranjestad (a small city on the northwest end of the island) named San Pedro. San Pedro's mission was to provide for the needs of the non-Exxon employees, i.e., the indigenous Arubans. My dad went to San Pedro on the weekends, on days when he had free time or in emergencies.

Aruba obtained its autonomy from Dutch rule and oversight in the early 1960s. Although Aruba was no longer under Dutch rule, the Queen of Holland had great influence. John van Ogtrop's service to the Exxon employees and the indigenous Arubans was not forgotten. On April 9, 1963, he was awarded a membership as an officer in the Order of Oranje Nassau, by order of the Queen of Holland, with many dignitaries in attendance. My Dad's award was for exemplary service to the medically needy in Aruba. The award is not limited to Dutch persons, as there are Americans in the U.S. who have also received the award.

My mom was very proud of "her John" but he thought it was not a big deal. Personally, I believe the bureaucrats at Exxon and in Aruba made a large mistake as alluded to earlier in the memoir.

My siblings can, if they read this memoir, come up with some other characteristics I have overlooked or not listed, but all seven of us would agree, we were very fortunate to have been the children of John and Martha and are the beneficiaries of their 1938 leap of faith to that little island in the Caribbean.

A Boy From Aruba

Back row, left to right: John, Dad, Mom, Piet, Muff (Maria)
Front row: Dick, Marca (Martha), Elsje (Elizabeth),
Patty (Patricia)

SIBLINGS – I am the eldest of Martha and John's children and every two years or so a new van Ogtrop child would make an appearance. I took for granted my new siblings until John and Martha decided seven was enough. Family pictures would portray proud parents and seven offspring. I never realized the importance to my parents of keeping all of us children as a cohesive unit and they reveled in taking family pictures. Since where we lived and were brought up was a small community and each of us had our own set of friends, interaction with siblings was not that important and we just lived our own lives.

As we left Aruba to come to the U.S. for college and to live our independent lives, it became apparent, at least to me, that my siblings were indeed a very important part of my life. While they each went their own way, married, had their own children and grandchildren, and did not need to be as close as in past years, time changed that. As the ravages of aging, health and time afflicted us, with various and sundry issues, we all came to realize that family is very important. Trips to Scientists' Cliffs, Sandy Island, pool parties and other family gatherings became very important and were looked forward to by all of us. Boxing Day gatherings were particularly special.

The passing of our younger sister, Marca, on November 20, 2022, after a long and painful five years with brain cancer, and the attendant gatherings and outpouring of love and admiration for each of us, made the blessing of family cohesiveness and caring, that which our folks instilled in us, a guiding principle in the van Ogtrop sibling family moving forward in life. I think John and Martha would approve of our relationships with each other, and our respective spouses and nephews and nieces. It is fun to be a vO.

We seven are all different, some fair-skinned, others dark-complexioned, with different political persuasions, different ball teams to root for, different annoying habits. Some are good athletes, some good spear fishermen, some good tennis players, some good golfers, etc., but with one commonality – we really care for each other and that is a blessing we continue to share, with disagreements periodically. What family in the U.S. does not have them, considering the topsy-turvy state of our governance. I was trying to not get political nonsense in this innocuous memoir, but I cannot help myself.

All seven siblings have longstanding marriages, we all received good American educations, we all had children, we were all successful in our chosen fields and there are many grandchildren. In general, we have led very charmed lives and I think our parents would be proud.

The three brothers

Siblings and spouses, Bethany Beach, 2021

Piet H. van Ogtrop

Chapter 20
Conclusion

I have had the good fortune to be married to my wife, Connie, for sixty-one-plus years. We have three very lovely daughters, three sons-in-law who were instrumental in bringing eight grandchildren (seven grandsons and one granddaughter) into the world and many nephews and nieces. My siblings' spouses are also very special to us.

Connie is a very talented and devoted wife, mother and grandmother. She took great care of our young daughters when I went to work, was involved with their school activities, took care of her mom, who had Alzheimer's and cared for her dad in his failing years. She taught school while I was in law school. She pursued and completed her master's degree at the University of Delaware and donated her master's thesis to Sloan Kettering for its use in cancer research. Connie had a private practice for some twenty years in nutritional assessment of her patients and behavior modification, and she also wrote a newsletter associated with her professional career.

Connie often volunteered in school activities for our children and was very much involved with me in my law practice as a solo practitioner on Delaware Avenue in Newark. For some ten years she was, in addition to maintaining her own practice on the second floor of my office building, my office manager, helping with organization, ordering supplies, checking bills and expenses, and particularly dealing with various secretaries.

She always loved doing yardwork and also designed and was the "general contractor" for two houses we built. She helped paint our homes on Kenyon Lane and 23 Mt. Airy Drive. Connie played both tennis and golf in her "spare time," as well as pursued her love of painting, which she continues to enjoy. The list of her many and varied accomplishments could go on and on.

This memoir will, most likely, be read by persons who know Connie and I could continue to expound on her accomplishments but will shorten my characterization of her, and to those who read this memoir, I believe their endorsement would follow.

She has been a loyal, caring, loving, interested and interesting person, proud and happy with her three daughters and their stations in life, full of love and admiration for her eight grandchildren, a good neighbor and friend. And for me, a great catch for a Dutch boy from the tropics. We have been a good team, she as the one who has kept the ship afloat and steering the ship on a good path.

I am proud to have had Connie at my side for all these years, and some health issues notwithstanding, hope our ship will continue to sail well.

I have been blessed with three lovely and talented daughters who no longer sail on our ship but are an integral part of the former crew. All three girls went to good colleges, did graduate work, worked in business, were a magazine editor, a CFO of a major retail corporation and have had a successful and rewarding career in personal counseling. They make me, as their father, very proud.

The five of us – Valerie's graduation

A Boy From Aruba

The days of working in a box factory during the summer, working in a drug store, cleaning my office and other assorted jobs created the impetus to put their talents to good use, and their work ethic is very strong.

The three girls are very different but also very similar. They are loyal, industrious, fun-loving, good athletes and have good senses of humor but different tastes regarding marriage partners and marriage ceremonies. Kristin (eldest) is married to Dean, who's serious, quiet, loves soccer, ultimate frisbee and is very smart. Kristin had a steel band at her wedding. Valerie (middle daughter) is married to Cooper, who's extroverted, loves University of Kansas sports, is a steak-and-potatoes guy, a good basketball player and loves life. Valerie had a band at her wedding, whose band leader was released from prison on her wedding day. Claire (youngest) is married to Gavin, a Connecticut Yankee who's very principled, hard working, stubborn, comfortable in his own domain, loves the outdoors, and is not afraid of hard work. Claire had a rockabilly band at her wedding. The girls each wished to have a pig roasted for their main entree. All weddings were enjoyable and the girls are still with their mates and have produced eight grandchildren, seven boys and one young lady. I have many nephews and nieces. Family gatherings on Boxing Day and at Sandy Island are great fun when van Ogtrops and progeny abound.

The grandchildren have gone their separate ways, into law, banking and teaching. Some are still in college and all are close to leaving home. Connie and I are very proud of the successes of our grandchildren.

Piet H. van Ogtrop

Grandchildren at Baby Beach in Aruba

I feel I have gone far afield in this memoir, but as I have been happy with my life, very happy and blessed with my life partner, very happy and blessed with my daughters and grandchildren and sons-in-law, I had to make my memoir complete.

In conclusion, a very special thanks to John and Martha for making the trip to the unknown in 1938 and giving the gift of a wonderful life to me and my siblings. My thanks are simple – a gift of a chance to live a life well lived.

Your son, Piet Hein

A Boy From Aruba

John and Martha's family

Piet H. van Ogtrop

Acknowledgment

My tennis friend, Jill Gomez, added a professional touch to this memoir through her insight, thoroughness, patience and countless hours of work, and her work product has made me a very proud and gratified author.

Many thanks to you, Jill.

Piet H. van Ogtrop

About the Author

Piet H. van Ogtrop was born in Aruba in 1939 to Dutch parents. He left Aruba in 1956 to attend John Carroll University in Cleveland, Ohio, and received his B.A. in 1960. He graduated from Dickinson Law School in Carlisle, Pennsylvania in 1963 and practiced law in Delaware for forty-eight years until retiring in 2012. He's married to Connie, his wife of sixty-one years. They have three married daughters, seven grandsons and one granddaughter. Piet and Connie live in State College, Pennsylvania.

A Boy From Aruba

Made in the USA
Middletown, DE
08 April 2024